# SUMMONS
## TO A HIGH
# CRUSADE

# SUMMONS
## TO A HIGH
# CRUSADE

## George Trevelyan

*april 1996*

*Happy Easter*

*to*

*Susie*

*Love*
*aunt Libbie*

### THE FINDHORN PRESS

ISBN 0 905249 64 X

First published 1986
Copyright © George Trevelyan

Set in 11/12 point Garamond by Findhorn Publications.
Book and cover design by Findhorn Foundation Design Group.
Printed and bound by Biddles Ltd, Guildford, UK.

Published by The Findhorn Press, The Park, Forres IV36 0TZ, Scotland.

# Contents

*A wind has blown across the world*
  *And tremors shake its frame*
*New things are struggling to their birth*
  *And naught shall be the same.*
*The Earth is weary of its past*
  *Of folly, hate and fear,*
*Beyond the dark and stormy sky*
  *The dawn of God is near.*

*A wind is blowing through the Earth*
  *A tempest loud and strong.*
*The trumpets of the Christ the King*
  *Thunder the skies along.*
*The summons to a high crusade*
  *Calling the brave and true*
*To find a New Jerusalem*
  *And build the world anew.*

*F.C. Happold*

# Foreword

By Peter Caddy

It gives me much pleasure to introduce this book by Sir George Trevelyan, the man whom, more than any other, I regard as the father of the new age in Britain. It was he who at Attingham Park Adult College in Shropshire initially drew together the key people in the new age spiritual movement in this country. There, in that delightful country-house setting where we immediately felt at home, many connections were made that were to bear fruit in the future.

It was he too who first put the Findhorn Community 'on the map' by sharing his observations and experience of the work being done in the community gardens with key people in groups such as the Soil Association, the Biodynamic Association and other organisations connected with gardening and horticulture. In his long association with the community many have been the times that he has stuck his neck out on its behalf, and his love, enthusiasm and personal support for myself are qualities I appreciate deeply.

He began the tradition of bringing together members and leaders of various groups and committees around Britain at an annual Round Table Conference—a gathering of friends to share what was happening in their fields. The whole atmosphere of love and harmony surrounding these events ensured that in Britain cooperation and not competition was the foundation of new age spiritual activity. Later a series of Round Table Gatherings were held in Europe to fulfil the same purpose on a broader field.

Not only was Sir George a Trustee of the Findhorn Foundation for many years but also, inspiring orator that he is, a popular speaker here, and he has given the opening talk at many of the community's conferences, his presence providing a point of inspiration, upliftment and effervescent fun and joy.

One of the highlights in the early years of his association with the Findhorn Community was his regular October workshop on *The Living Word*, where among other things up-and-coming community speakers learnt the mastery of 'the pregnant pause'.

Sir George's forte is indeed the *living* word. The written word can only partially capture the impact that he makes on an audience through his vitality, love, inspiration and vision. But those qualities come through all he does. I commend this book to you.

Peter Caddy

# Preface

This book offers a series of lectures which I gave at the Findhorn Foundation over a ten year period. It became almost a tradition for me to give the opening talk at many of the conferences. This honourable tradition came about through a warm connection with the Community, which I first visited in 1968. There were then 15 members and I remember lunching in April sun outside Joannie Hartnell-Beavis' bungalow among glowing great daffodils, broad leaved trees and magnificent vegetables. Now, I know this area of Scotland well, through having taught at Gordonstoun. This arid coastal strip of sand dunes grew nothing but spikey grass, gorse and occasional fir trees. Yet here was I in a luxuriant garden, fed on the best vegetables I had ever tasted. It was clearly not enough to accept Peter Caddy's explanation about compost and hard work. I knew that another factor must be at work and I knew from my experience of Steiner's biodynamic horticulture what that Factor X must be. Here was direct contact with the elemental world of the nature spirits. Caddy had broken through into direct cooperation with these living energies. I pressed him and for the first time he publicly admitted the truth and told the whole story. So I wrote a memorandum to my friend Lady Eve Balfour of the Soil Association, urging her to come and see what was happening in northern Scotland and to bring her soil experts. The story is written in *The Findhorn Garden*. I am proud to have been instrumental in making this link.

Peter had come to me in 1964 at Attingham, the Shropshire Adult College, of which I was Principal. That story is told in *The Magic of Findhorn* by Paul Hawken. I had arranged a conference on 'Groups in the New Age', and Eileen Caddy had had dawn guidance which said, "Peter will know whether he is to go to Attingham." He knew—but none of them knew where or what Attingham was! So they looked it up on the map and he leaped into his car with another person and pounded down the length of Britain. On the way down, he called on a friend who urged him to telephone, since all beds for such a conference would have been booked up for weeks ahead and, anyway, it was by invitation only. My secretary, Ruth Bell, came to me to say, "There's a chap from Scotland on the phone who says he's running a community and that he's coming with one other. What shall we do?" My reaction

10

was right—to let him come. And sure enough, another voice spoke shortly over the telephone to cancel two beds because the driver had gone down with 'flu! That evening occurred the amusing incident when Air Marshal Sir Victor Goddard turned to Peter and asked, "Would you explain to us your financial policy in your community." I remember Peter rolling his eyes, taking a deep breath and declaring: "You give everything to God, give thanks that your needs will be met and then the necessary supply comes." Those early heroic days of the Findhorn Community truly demonstrated the Laws of Manifestation.

So after my visit in 1968 I came every year to take part in the conferences. I was never a member of the Community, for I was fully engaged in running Attingham and, after retirement in 1971, the Wrekin Trust, which promotes conferences and courses on spiritual knowledge in adult education. But my connection with the Findhorn Community was very close and warm, and in due course I was asked to join the Trustees under the chairmanship of Captain Ross Stewart, R.N. Trustees' meetings were indeed remarkable gatherings. So the custom began of my giving the opening talk for almost all of the conferences at Findhorn. I felt greatly privileged to have this opportunity. It was a great moment when the Universal Hall was completed and we held the first conference in that noble pentagon. Here let me record an amusing incident. Talking with Peter in the early days, I urged the need for building a theatre. It became clear to us that the site should be on the dunes outside The Park building. Two or three of us went out to consider the possibility and I remember leaping on to a sandy rise and beginning to declaim some passage from Shakespeare. Unknown to me Peter had come up quietly beside me, when I made some sweeping arm gesture and struck him across the chest, knocking him over. Like William the Conqueror stumbling and biting the dust as he landed on the coast of England, Peter had been struck down on the site of the Universal Hall.

That Hall has been the scene for many fine lectures and creative, artistic events and demonstrations. It has for me been a delight and an honour to have had the chance to give this series of lectures. They are now published by The Findhorn Press, and I use this occasion to express my deep gratitude for all the companionship, joy and love which my connection with the Community has brought me over the years. This has been a vital factor in my life.

George Trevelyan

# Introduction
# Trailing Clouds of Glory

By Jeremy Slocombe

*This interview with Sir George appeared originally in the Australian magazine,* Simply Living, *Vol.2, No.1.*

When Sir George casually informed me that the room was full of angels, I wondered for a moment whether someone had tampered with the herbal teas.

He is, after all, a distinguished man, as happily resident in *Who's Who* as he is in *Burke's Peerage*. His adult life began as a craftsman in the Cotswold furniture tradition, and he was also one of the first qualified teachers of the Alexander Technique; he turned to formal education and during the war was a master at Gordonstoun, the princes' school. Later he became a pioneer of adult education in Britain, for 24 years Warden of the famous Attingham Park Adult College in Shropshire.

Angels or not, he brought a powerful presence to the room. Long, white hair and a bristle of moustache frame a face of animate intelligence; arthritis has cupped his hands as if they once had held the Holy Grail and were unwilling to forget the experience (nature cures and kindred therapies have prevented the arthritis spreading beyond his hands). These he now put to good use around a pottery mug of the tea in question.

"Don't be frightened by the word 'angels'," he continued. "It is simply a name given to energies which are alive. Not just mechanical, but live and operative thought-energies; *creative* energies. The room's full of them. An interview like this will have drawn them. I can't see them, probably you can't, but I know it's true."

That explained, he sat back and studied my response, like Gandalf teasing a Baggins with smoke rings.

Sir George's career rivals that of his famous uncle, the historian G.M. Trevelyan, with one important difference. G.M. won plaudits for his study of the past; nephew George lectures and writes about the

future and in 1982 was joint winner (with his Wrekin Trust) of the Right Livelihood Award, sometimes called the Alternative Nobel Prize. This, as its name implies, is an inspired attempt to credit outstanding contributions to the formulation of a new world view.

Sir George calls his the 'holistic' world view. We are, he says, recovering the knowledge—the conviction, in a sense—that life is a vast unity: that the universe is not a mechanism but an affair of mind, and it works as one huge harmony.

"As you grasp this concept, inevitably it leads to trying to live it. This is the phenomenon today. There is a real turning to new lifestyles. People are beginning to look forward to the future with excitement, and that's what matters. I know a number who have given up good and effective jobs in the cities and moved out into the hills of Wales to live an alternative lifestyle while so many others are looking to the future with alarm and despair and gloom and fear and doubt. *That's* the excitement: so many are breaking through into grasping the great oneness of things.

"We stand on a threshold where human consciousness can take a quantum leap out of self-consciousness into all-consciousness, God-consciousness. This has at all periods happened with some individuals. We have to remember that the phenomenon of the mystics, the initiates, the Illuminati is one that the intellectual mind cannot understand; but its appearance in history has set what is happening now.

"This consciousness includes the capacity to be one with any other being. Normally you and I experience separation: we are separate beings, which is the essence of Newtonian thinking. When I look into your eyes, however, I realise that it isn't just two chaps. The divinity in

15

me is the same as the divinity in you. Obviously: the holistic viewpoint implies it. I can look through your eyes and it is the divinity in me looking at itself through you. In this sense, we are one."

His blue eyes mirrored the wonderment in mine. I thought: these ideas are not an old man's fancy. They flow from years of scholarship and a search for truth which has made Sir George one of the greatest living authorities on the spiritual aspirations of our times.

He has not always dealt easily with angels. Until 36 he remained agnostic, preferring to hold "the rational, analytical, materialistic concept that man is an accident in a nature wholly indifferent to him." His conversion came during a lecture on the teachings of the German mystic, Rudolf Steiner: "I suddenly thought, 'My God, that's it!' The universe finally made sense to me."

He began introducing spiritual themes into his adult education courses, inviting and talking with different spiritual leaders and groups. This conversation slowly confirmed a suspicion he had formed during his scholarship, particularly in his study of English mystics like Blake and Wordsworth: that Britain, nay the world itself, was approaching the dawn of a new age of understanding and relationships.

This 'new age' was marked by the emergence of a new hierarchy of values which would impart a sense of deeper meaning to life in a difficult age. Sir George realised that the world problems created by human beings—like ecological imbalance and the nuclear threat—were already insoluble on a human level. He concluded, however, that a higher power was ready, like the US cavalry in the last reel of a dismal B-grade movie, to charge in and save the situation: if enough people recognised it and cried for help.

Sir George was excited by the evidence that this awareness was growing. Attingham Park became an unofficial headquarters of the move-

16

ment, as psychics, scholars, seers and scientists all contributed their particular pieces of a puzzle which, as it was assembled, suggested a remarkably uniform view of the human condition.

Sir George tells the tale with great gusto. "We're going back to what the Greeks knew, which is that all the secrets of the universe are hidden within the human organism and its evolution. The human body is a mobile temple into which a spiritual being can descend; we are each of us spiritual beings. The 'I' in us is an imperishable drop of divinity and therefore free from sense and body. It's a most terrific thought!

"Earth is the training ground to which we've descended in order to go through this long evolution to become, ultimately, in freedom, co-creators with God. This involves the process of an immortal spiritual being embedding itself deeper and deeper into the physical realm—through many lives, if you can take the idea—in order to achieve the point where it is, in a human sense, free. This is the point we've got to get: a being who's closely in touch with the angelic worlds would know that it is simply part of the whole will of God; not until we have been cut off from that can we really experience freedom.

"At a certain stage, when our true being gets identified with the five senses and the physical brain, the world of spirit disappears for us. This happened after the time of Newton. Spirit wasn't visible any more in the world or in nature and even the existence of God was thrown into doubt.

"This was a risk that had to be taken by the higher worlds: they had to let humans go and lose themselves in materialism, which could mean losing them completely. There is nothing wrong with materialism, however, let us be quite clear; it has benefited us enormously. It is the destiny of the West, particularly of the Anglo-Saxon races, to enter deep into the world of matter and master it. This was a

17

wonderful thing, but it did carry the risk that some of humankind would become so involved in matter that they would permanently lose a sense of the higher worlds.

"That is the critical point we have now reached. We have analysed matter so deeply that we've discovered that it's all energy. We are in the process of discovering that this energy is alive and that it's really a question of thought. Now it becomes part of the human adventure to step beyond the limitations of sense-bound consciousness into what we could call sense-free thinking. There is nothing to stop us expanding human consciousness into the great ocean of thought of which our minds are really strands.

"This is a great leap in consciousness which all of us should be concerned with. It is a form of different space exploration. We have developed physical space exploraton—there's nothing to stop us colonising the universe—but the shooting of rockets or building of space stations is still in the physical realm. We're appalled by the thought of the light years to the stars and how do we ever get to them—the terrifying scale of things—but the other form of space exploration is moving inwards and across the frontiers of thought into what must be called 'ethereal space'.

"This is best put by our great new age prophet, Blake, that the task is 'to open the Eternal Worlds, to open the Immortal Eyes of man inwards, into the Realms of Thought, into Eternity, ever expanding in the Bosom of God, the Human Imagination'.

"When you move into that inner world you are freed from the grave of the gravity world and can expand indefinitely. All the fear about light years and the size of the physical universe ceases to be important. On an ethereal level, you can be in Sirius—whoosh!—just like that, because you are outside time. That is the world the mystics enter and Blake was a master of it."

Strong stuff, which Sir George delivers with equally strong conviction. It is more than a tale cobbled together from the shards of Eastern mysticism, however; subscribers to the holistic world view now include some of the world's leading scientists who are, in Sir George's words, 'thinking' their way into the same concepts which the mystical tradition has held for centuries.

Prominent among these is Professor David Bohm, a physicist considered by many to be Einstein's natural successor. At the end of the last decade, Bohm published a book called *Wholeness and the Implicate Order*, which argued that everything in the universe, animate and in-

18

animate, is directly connected to everything else in one vast, unified field of energy. One could indeed not 'stir a flower without troubling of a star'.

A couple of years ago, Bohm took part in a conference organised by Sir George and the Wrekin Trust called 'Mystics and Scientists'. Bringing the two streams together is typical of the thoroughness with which Sir George marshalls his evidence: it is harder to resist the allure of angels when their existence can be neatly deduced from a mass of formulae on a blackboard.

Elsewhere in Britain he found what seemed like evidence of a more substantial kind. In 1965 he invited leaders of new age groups throughout the country to a gathering at Attingham Park. Among them came a brash, former RAF squadron leader called Peter Caddy, who claimed to be demonstrating in his fledgling community what the others were still talking about. "This was fighting talk," Sir George recalls, and he was determined to see this place for himself. Three years later he made his first visit to the Findhorn Foundation in the north of Scotland.

Those were the days when the Findhorn Community garden was producing, in virtual beach sand, the fat vegetables which were later to grow into legend. Sir George, a member of the Soil Association, knew that organic methods alone could not account for the splendid growth of the garden. He pressed Caddy for an explanation.

Eileen Caddy, Peter's wife, had been prepared for this moment by a message she had 'received' in her daily meditation: it was time to let the secret out. Peter Caddy told Sir George that they were working in direct communication with the 'devas'—angels—which animate the nature kingdom.

Sir George was impressed: after all, the results of that experiment were everywhere to be seen (and, presumably, eaten). He wrote a glowing report to Lady Eve Balfour, the Soil Association's founder, and thus set into motion the arrival of those soil experts whose testimony later placed the Findhorn Community firmly on the map of spiritual Britain.

What was happening at the Findhorn Foundation began to happen elsewhere. Groups of people were coming together in small communities and meditation circles and consciously seeking to contact and work with a superhuman stream of intelligence—whatever they called it. Sir George recognised a startling unity in the diversity of their techniques and terminology and devoted much of his time to visiting them and putting them in touch with one another.

In 1971 he retired from Attingham to concentrate on strengthening this network. He founded the Wrekin Trust, an educational charity 'dedicated to exploring the spirituality of man and the universe'; he also became a trustee of the Findhorn Foundation. He has written several books, including *A Vision of the Aquarian Age* and *Operation Redemption*, and started travelling further afield, to Europe, the States and South Africa; everywhere he goes, he proclaims the new age like some Mosaic cheerleader for the promised land. (During one of the annual Festivals of Mind, Body and Spirit in London—a smorgasbord of all things alternative—he seized a loaf of bread and flourished it for the benefit of the television cameras: "Wholewheat bread!" he declared, as if addressing the Sacrament, "the *whole* of the wheat!")

He fervently believes that there is an initiative required from us to expand our consciousness, through whichever technique works best, to allow the higher worlds to work with us and rescue the world from assured self-destruction. "If the mere rationalist intellect is in control alone, nothing's going to stop someone pushing that damn button. We're in for it. So—we've got to call on the angels, the forces of light. The moment we do that—well, as the angels are there to obey the will of God and we are divine in our essence, it is valid that we can give them the orders.

"This is the power behind the change that's coming now. People can be frightened by the darkness and the violence and how terrible the world looks, but they should realise that behind it is all the transforming power of the world of light, which could change anything. It could even effect molecular change—as enough human beings lift their consciousness in prayer, meditation and invocation.

"I come back to this very important point, that we have been allowed to develop to freedom and free choice. We've had to achieve that freedom by being cut off and going through centuries of separation. This is all part of a plan to create—dare I say—a hierarchy of spiritual beings, a little lower than the angels, who can carry free will and therefore potentially become co-creators with God: nothing less than that. Don't be put off by the terminology, all this talk of God and angels. The scientists are saying the same thing and using different words for it.

"The holistic picture implies that the Earth is a living creature. We are the point at which nature has become self-conscious, the part where the Earth is looking out into the cosmos from herself. Can I quote Coleridge?

*. . .we receive but what we give,* Coleridge
*And in our life alone does Nature live:*
*Ours is her wedding garment, ours her shroud!*

In other words, *we* make nature dead or alive.

*Ah! from the soul itself must issue forth*
*A light, a glory, a fair luminous cloud*
*Enveloping the Earth—*
*And from the soul itself must there be sent*
*A sweet and potent voice, of its own birth,*
*Of all sweet sounds the life and element!*

"This new birth comes when, with our imaginative consciousness, we take a step out of our separation into wholeness, which we are open to do perfectly safely. The soul can project light. In your imagination, you can come outside the Earth and see it like a soccer ball in front of you—obviously you can—and then wrap that in light.

"When you do that in your imagination, you have to have the courage to think you really are building something on the higher, etheric plane. You are gifting this creation to the higher world, and as enough do it, we release a power. Those poets of the Romantic Movement knew that nature is not fulfilled till human beings take the step in consciousness to discover the being within form and nature."

At this point I interrupted Sir George and asked his opinion of the growing peace movements around the world, many of which combine imaginative exercises of this sort with more down to earth political agitation. Were they, too, an expression of the new consciousness? His eyebrows bristled. "We're not concerned with the politics of the thing, let's not touch them at all.

"What we are seeing is a tremendous human phenomenon: the real human being (which is a spiritual being too, remember) is realising that the taking of life, the spilling of blood is intolerable. Now this is not only our discovery. Perhaps I'm jumping too far, but let's say it: there is a supreme hope that, ultimately, the divine world is not going to allow us to destroy the life of a planet. We are the first generation that has the ability to do so.

"I've said that the angelic world won't interfere to the detriment of our freedom, but there are certain things—if they are going to be detrimental to the whole organism of the solar system—that we may

21

not do. Remember that the holistic picture implies that everything is organism and alive: the Earth is alive, but you don't get a living organism in the middle of a dead mechanism. The Earth and the planets are comparable to the endocrine glands of the body. If one of those goes sick, the whole body's sick. Well, now, the whole body of the solar system is going sick through Earth's going dead.

"Do you honestly think that the divine hierarchies are going to sit back and let the galaxies be damaged by our selfishness and ignorance destroying the life on this planet? I don't think they will. Here is the real dramatic hope: if we really came to the Armageddon, releasing all these nuclear weapons, what we're going to find is that the damn things won't work. We will find that these higher streams of intelligence have the capacity to instantly negate any nuclear device. The rockets will just dissolve or dematerialise.

"I would say this now: if the materialists are right, if there is nothing more than rational materialism, it is no good their saying, 'Oh come off all this apocalyptic sort of talk, let's be sensible people and get over this sort of thing and it will probably improve the economics.' The problem is already insoluble by human self-sufficiency. The deterrent must, one day, fail to deter. If that's not sensational, if that's not dramatic, I don't know what is: the killing of 90% of the Earth's population before breakfast. Well, my God!

"Therefore it's much more fun, may I say, to look apocalyptically at it and see this sublime possibility that the divine worlds could neutralise them. It's a terrific idea!"

His words exploded in my brain like one of the ghastly weapons in his monologue: I had never before associated the words 'fun' and 'Armageddon'. I mumbled something about such an event having a traumatic effect on the established theocracies. We would no longer need priestly intermediaries to plead for the existence of God.

"Yes—quite," said Sir George. "We would be on our knees: God immanent and we not dead! This is the vital importance of our establishing the link with the higher worlds now; that they may be empowered to do whatever they can do then.

"When I talk about this in my lectures, there is a rustle of excitement over the audience: 'My God, this is exciting, this is thrilling, this is fun!' and, as the world is so mad and so bad and so dangerous, well! Let's have the excitement of counter-thinking: that a transformation could be coming, that the change will change everything. Of course it's outrageous, but the world is outrageous!

"We are now waking up to ourselves; and to the fact that there is this ultimate, complete energy which is the united intelligence of the cosmos. All this new age movement is not just somebody's thought-out plan for a better society. It is a spiritual awakening to the reality of something greater beyond us.

" Having grasped the holistic world view—that we are spiritual beings in a life that is a vast oneness, that the Earth is alive and we are its stewards—having grasped that as a concept, an intellectual theory, it at once becomes totally inappropriate that I should blow your brains out, for instance...."

Here the cassette recorder snapped off suddenly, its tape run out. Sir George embraced me affectionately and was gone. Overhead I heard not the rustle of angels departing but the roar of Vulcan bombers on manoeuvres from a nearby RAF base.

I was left with a verse from another of Sir George's favourite poems, Wordsworth's *Intimations of Immortality:*

> *Our birth is but a sleep and a forgetting:*
> *The Soul that rises with us, our life's Star,*
> *Hath had elsewhere its setting,*
> *And cometh from afar:*
> *Not in entire forgetfulness,*
> *And not in utter nakedness,*
> *But trailing clouds of glory do we come*
> *From God, who is our home:*
> *Heaven lies about us in our infancy!*
> *Shades of the prison-house begin to close*
> *Upon the growing Boy,*
> *But He beholds the light, and whence it flows,*
> *He sees it in his joy;*
> *The Youth, who daily further from the east*
> *Must travel, still is Nature's Priest,*
> *And by the vision splendid*
> *Is on his way attended;*
> *At length the Man perceives it die away,*
> *And fade into the light of common day.*

I felt the sadness of that closing couplet. The rational mind, the roof chatter of the brain, returned to voice its annoyance at what seemed the simplistic optimism of Sir George's message: that it is up to us to revive the 'vision splendid'. Yet a deeper doubt remained. As I re-wound the cassette to hear his words again, I thought it would not be possible to go back and discover what we had missed, if the thin tape of our life on Earth snapped off as brusquely.

# Chapter One
# Summons to a High Crusade

*'Peace Within' Gathering, New Year's Eve, 1983*

This last great night of the year is a major event in the cycle of the living Earth as it pauses in the magical period of the twelve holy nights. The whole of nature is waiting in suspense, almost as if once again it needs permission from the heights to move into the growth and activity that leads to spring. Feel this absolute stillness. How right it is that we go into either meditation or celebration to bring in the new year. What matters is to feel that we are taking part in a cosmic celebration. Ring out the old, ring in the new... ring in the Christ that is to be.

What is this world about which we are so desperately concerned? Consider these words by the 13th-century mystic Meister Eckhardt: "All that man has here externally, in multiplicity, is intrinsically one. Here all blades of grass and stones—all things—are one. This is the deepest depth, and thereby I am completely captivated."

A modern expression of the same theme comes from Roger Lindquist: "Many fine silk threads together creating the great tapestry of life, the supreme thread, the great Tao, inspiring the ten thousand things into existence, that they may reflect the inexhaustible depth and subtlety, become one with its all-embracing essence. All things interacting in an ever-changing continuity, determined equally by the changeless immovable centre, the still point whence the cosmic dance originates from moment to moment."

This is the consciousness we are dealing with—that peak experience when the human being breaks through from normal separative self-consciousness into cosmic consciousness. It is the noetic experience: the direct, immediate and certain experience of reality as a great oneness. We are all reaching the threshold where we overcome the limitations of sense-bound, brain-bound consciousness, when mind in us unites with Universal Mind. This is the immense excitement of the time we live in.

In the light of that vision, what do we make of the terrifying picture we are given of the world today? It is important to remember that the whole universe is alive and is the vast thought of God. The Book of Genesis starts with: "In the beginning God created heaven and earth." But the Essene Book of Creation, the counterpart to Genesis, says: "Without beginning, the Law creates life and thought." In other words, there is a perpetual spring of virgin thought and new life streaming from the divine source, without beginning and without end. While our world appears to be running down in massive entropy, eternal life is flooding out into a great ocean of thought, intelligence and creative idea.

From that, we come to the concept of angelic hierarchies. Angels are simply the name we give to strands of the thought of God which are so alive that they are beings, ranging through the nine great hierarchies from the Elohim and Seraphim down to the invisible beings who have the task of looking after us. Our imagination is called upon to grasp that there are levels of intelligence up and up to the God source, at higher and higher frequencies. We ourselves have been called the tenth hierarchy, spiritual beings incarnated upon this Earth in heavy, solid matter; dense bodies embedded in the sense world with a very low vibratory rate. The five senses enable us to operate in this world, and they are also filters to protect us. "Humankind cannot bear very much reality," said T.S. Eliot. And in the poem *The Cage* Martin Armstrong says: "Man, afraid to be alive, shuts his soul in senses five."

The challenge is now for us to dare to come out into the greater world. We are crossing a frontier and starting on a form of space exploration—an exploration of interior space opening into ethereal space, an exploration of thought and creative imagination that takes us over the entire universe. We are asked to move into the realms of creative being and to embrace a holistic world view where creative Ideas—Beings—are poured forth from the God Mind and expressed, pressed forth, into physical form. The amazing artistry of nature—flowers, trees, rocks, crystals, birds, animals and humanity itself—is a picture of that world.

The whole is a great oneness in all its diversity, and there are many levels of intelligence. Every visible body is the creation of Idea. The sun itself, an apparently gaseous body, is really a structure enabling the highest spiritual beings to operate. There is a spiritual sun behind the physical sun. Blake, that great seer, knew this well. "When the sun rises," he said, "do you think that I see something rather like a golden guinea in the sky? No, no, no, I see and hear an innumerable company of the heavenly host singing *Glory be to God on High.*" He could see straight through the physical sun into the spiritual sun.

The Lord of the Spiritual Sun, of the Elohim and Seraphim, is he whom we call the Christos, and who now overlights our planet. That Cosmic Christ saw it right to move down and enter the stream of Earth existence, to be the one God to experience human death. In the end, he took possession of the entire life force of the Earth. Seen esoterically, the ascension of the risen Christ to heaven is an upward movement into the etheric body of the planet, to the higher frequency of the etheric world. He says: "I am with you always, even to the end of the Earth cycle," and is therefore the divine being present in every plant, tree, bird and animal, and in every human heart. The whole of the etheric life force is the habitation of the vast being of the Christ.

We must realise that intelligence is creative on all levels. We believe there can be no life on Venus because it is so hot that it would just burn up. But do you see how limited that thinking is? What we mean is: could *this* body live on Venus? But this body is a temple, a protective sheath enabling a spiritual being to descend to Earth. Since we are on a rocky planet we need a sheath with the heavy density of Earth, a solid skeleton which can enable us to operate as human beings. If we were to incarnate on a viscous, watery planet, we should need a fishy body; on a gaseous planet, a gaseous body; or on a flaming planet like the sun, a flame body.

It is conceivable that there are all sorts of places where civilisations can exist. It has been said that 'in my Father's house are many mansions'. In a universe of ever higher intelligence, a whole city could exist in what we call 'space', totally invisible to us because our senses are attuned simply to the physical. Right now, for instance, sound waves of Beethoven, jazz and many other things are constantly coming through this room, but because we are not attuned to them and have no instrument to pick them up, we are completely unaware of these sounds. There can also be planets, civilisations and architecture throughout space that are invisible to us. The whole of creation is filled with intelligence far ahead of ours. We are not the highest level of intelligence—we are simply a high point in Earth evolution. But on Earth humanity is that conscious point in nature which can now in freedom take over responsibility for evolution. Instead of evolution being merely a force which shapes and evolves forms, it is a force which is handed over to us, reminding us that we have free choice to make the world we choose.

Through evolution we are working towards the primal human archetype: a spiritual, universal being made in God's image. Our potential is absolutely unlimited. As the sons and daughters of God, we are widening and extending, and there is nothing to stop us from expanding into the greater whole. Ours is the generation to do this. We stand at the razor's edge, to take over conscious evolution. Self-consciousness, egoism, greed and ignorance have brought us to the point where we can destroy the whole planet and all life on it. Alternatively, we can move forward into a future far more wonderful than is possible for us to imagine. The choice is ours. Which are we going to choose?

Remember to think holistically. The Earth is not just a dead mineral but a living and breathing organism with the equivalent of its own feeling, thinking, bloodstream, glands and consciousness. We are the microcosm; the Earth is the macrocosm. The mere fact that we can breathe and have a bloodstream and endocrine glands means that the macrocosm does too.

But it does not end there. There cannot be a living organism in the middle of a dead mechanism. The entire solar system is also a living organism with the sun as its heart and each of the planets as an endocrine gland. A gland is a focalising point for the life forces in the body, and if one of our endocrine glands gets sick our whole body becomes ill, and we have to do something about it. In the planetary solar body one of the planets, a gland, has become lamentably sick and threatens to extinguish life upon itself. How long do we think the higher intelligence of the solar system is going to tolerate this sickness? The answer, quite clearly, is no longer.

An operation to heal and cleanse the planet has been launched. For the last ten years a power which is best called love—a very high frequency of light and harmony—has been pouring into the world of matter and raising its frequency rate. As human beings are part of the world of matter, our own frequency rate is rising. We are on the threshold of fourth and fifth dimensional consciousness. Change is taking place.

The paradox is that humanity has been given freedom. This lovely planet is our training ground and operation base, and we are to become co-creators with God. It is as if the Great Creator wanted something in his wonderful creation that could itself start creating. He wanted to be able to look down and exclaim: "Look, what a thrill! Look what they are doing on our little planet Earth!" Imagine the angels watching and saying: "Look, they've done something we never thought of. They have really begun to make something new." As humanity begins to be creative, the whole is enriched. And God too is enriched, for everything always works as a whole. This is the immense endeavour we are involved in.

This planet is so important that it was considered worthy of the highest being of the Spiritual Sun to descend and go through death—a very high compliment. We try to write off the human race as a chance natural selection, but how ludicrous that is. We are the great experiment of God, given freedom which may not be violated. The angels are working with us, but certainly the archangels dealing with them must have briefed them: "Go and train your men and women down there, but under no conditions are you to interfere with their freedom."

We ourselves do something similar with our children, seeking to educate them and give them all the freedom we can. But if, for instance, the children decide to have a bonfire in the drawing room, we should say: "No, I will not allow that. Go and have your fun elsewhere." That would not really be a serious limitation of freedom! Similarly there are points beyond which *we* may not go. Do you honestly think it is likely that in the living organism of the solar system, which is part of the living organism of the galaxy, the Divine Word is going to fold its hands and sit by, saying, "I suppose if they really want to blow themselves up we had better let them. We must not violate their freedom." The whole situation is absurd. We have created something so monstrous, so ridiculous, so fantastic and so mad that we can hardly expect the levels of higher intelligence to tolerate what we are proposing to risk doing.

"What God has joined together let no man put asunder." This saying is conventionally applied to the marriage service. But what God has also joined together is the nuclear centre, and the taking apart of the centre in the atom is an obscene achievement which has nothing to do with life. It is life-destroying and therefore inexcusable. At this point it is valid for higher intelligence to intervene. Many communications coming through from the higher levels of angelic intelligence imply that it is unthinkable that humanity be allowed to destroy life upon the planet. If we come to the point of pressing that button, they will intervene. They have said, in effect, that their intelligence is so far ahead of our elementary electronics that they would have no difficulty in instantly neutralising any nuclear device. Further, they claim to be monitoring our planet, invisible to us, with millions of spaceships. They are closely watching all we are doing, and are invisibly present in all our counsels, military discussions, cabinet and Kremlin meetings.

I am not asking you to believe any of this. These statements about the spiritual world cannot be proven with the senses. Science has been built on the doctrine that it is not valid to believe anything that cannot be proven in this way. But the result is we have cut ourselves off from the living whole, from the super-sensible world we are now exploring.

However, if these ideas appeal to you, I invite you to take them and put them in your thinking and your heart, to live and act as if you believe in them and to look at life in light of them. An idea is a living being, and if it is true it will draw certainty to itself as you live with it, until you simply *know* it is true. On this planet we have created problems which are already insoluble by human self-sufficiency alone. Communications from higher sources have said many times that if we continue thinking in terms of separation we will never solve them. But if we can shift our consciousness to work with the whole, then all these problems can be solved.

In one communication the archangel Gabriel said: "The army shall be stopped by a great natural cataclysm. The weapons shall melt in their hands. They will find finally that the Earth has reached the place where the vibrations will no longer tolerate the act of wanton murder on the part of its inhabitants. For centuries man has spilled blood upon the Earth; now the vibration refuses to kill. In the great war when man raises his weapons against his fellow man, they will not function. In the new vibration, anything that will cause destruction will melt. If a man utters a destructive word, he will disintegrate. Everything negative will vanish."

It is all perfectly possible. The great hope now is if that button is pushed, it will be the signal not for the downwards release of uncontrolled destruction but rather the upwards release of the living energy within the nuclear centre. That energy is ultimately Christ himself. He is present now not only in the etheric but right in the nuclear centre. Is he really likely to allow himself to be used to finish off his entire experiment? Because he is everywhere in every one of these centres, is it not more likely that the explosion will result in a vast manifestation of light filling the heavens, truly the 'blinding light' of initiation? May this be the meaning of the apocalyptic phrase: "After the tribulation cometh the Son of Man upon the clouds of heaven with power and great glory and the trumpeting of angels"?

Now you can see what an adventure we are living through. When we are on the brink of nuclear war and at the point of absolute despair, have we the courage to remember that then the wonder will happen? In the twinkling of an eye the change could come about.

We cannot be complacent. The world today is a dangerous and dramatic place, and it seems that the pushing of the button is inevitable sooner or later. So what do we do? If rational, materialistic thinking is right, then let us eat, drink and be merry, for tomorrow we die—by the million! But it is not the only truth. Rather let us put our bottom dollar on the superb concept that we are working with a divine power that would have no difficulty in neutralising the bomb. A flash of divine thought could bring about molecular change which could de-pollute the planet. This is the scale of the times we are living in. If you know this you will realise that the crisis we are working up to is one of immense joy. The planet is moving into a new age, and we have our part to play in the mighty drama.

*A wind has blown across the world*
*And tremors shake its frame*
*New things are struggling to their birth*
*And naught shall be the same.*
*The Earth is weary of its past*
*Of folly, hate and fear,*
*Beyond the dark and stormy sky*
*The dawn of God is near.*

*A wind is blowing through the Earth*
*A tempest loud and strong.*
*The trumpets of the Christ the King*
*Thunder the skies along.*
*The summons to a high crusade*
*Calling the brave and true*
*To find a New Jerusalem*
*And build the world anew.* *

This is what we are involved in, dear friends.

*F.C. Happold

# Chapter Two
# The Myth of the Human Soul

*Spring Festival of the Arts, Easter 1985*

Dear friends, it seems appropriate on Easter Sunday to begin with
Spenser's great Easter sonnet:

> *Most glorious Lord of Life that, on this day,*
> *Did'st make Thy triumph over death and sin;*
> *And, having harrowed hell, did'st bring away*
> *Captivity thence captive, us to win.*
> *This joyous day, deare Lord, with joy begin;*
> *And grant that we, for whom Thou diddest dye*
> *Being by Thy deare blood clene washt from sin*
> *May live for ever in felicity!*
> *And that Thy love we weighing worthily*
> *May likewise love Thee for the same againe;*
> *And for Thy sake, that all lyke deare did'st buy*
> *With love may one another entertayne!*
> *So let us love, dear Love, lyke as we ought,*
> *Love is the lesson that the Lord us taught.*

Let us stretch our thinking. I invite you to come on an imaginative
journey. Look first at your own body, this point of consciousness. Look
at the Earth through the point of your body. Realise your body as a sen-
sitised point of the living Earth. See the powers of the field of gravity
focalised into that sensitive point. Right at the outset, overcome the
sense that we are separated and merely observers of nature. That is the
hurdle we must first get over. We *are* nature; we are that point where
nature becomes conscious of itself. Experience your own body as a
point given over to the field of gravity—and then come out into the
opposite polarity.

Leave that body and rise so that you float above the Earth. Look at that beautiful Earth. You remain linked with your body but you are already experiencing the great polarity between gravity and levity, between the pull to the centre of the Earth and the draw from the vast circumference. Experience, therefore, falling upwards. Feel the buoyant, expansive power of spirit lifting into ethereal space. You are not merely in physical space. You are not playing at being a rocket; you are, in fact, moving into another reality. The rocket is simply something pushed up. We are talking about the great polarity of gravity and levity, the pull to the point in the centre and the counter-pull to the great periphery, noting that this has been overlooked since the time of Newton. Human consciousness in its intellectual materialism has lost the realisation of the true polarity of gravity and its counter, levity. In this very simple experiment you are lifting and realising that you are a being of both of these. Where are you now? Where is your consciousness? Certainly not in the point of your body, which you have left down there.

You grasp this great truth, that your consciousness is not in your body, but your body is in your consciousness. Your consciousness is wherever in ethereal space you choose to project it—instantly. You now experience your body as a focalised point which enables you as a spiritual being to touch down and operate in the heavy density of the world of matter. The real 'you' is immortal and universal and is wherever it directs its attention. And even so simple and imaginative a meditation as this can give you that experience. We are exploring ethereal space and realising the design of this body temple—for a temple is what it is, divinely designed to enable a universal spiritual being to operate on this dense plane, employing the divine faculties of thought, love and creative volition.

Now look down upon the globe of the Earth. See it in all its beauty, and at one step get over that conception of a few generations ago that humans are an accident of chance natural selection in a nature completely indifferent to them—a point of view wholly inadequate to explain the wonder of the universe and humankind. "What, then, is man that Thou art mindful of him and the Son of man that Thou visitest him, for Thou hast made him a little lower than the angels and crowned him with glory and honour."

Look at that planet. Now grasp the concept of what we really are. Humanity collectively is in the process of becoming the brain and nervous system of the living organism of the planet. Grasp the idea that the planet is a living creature with its own breathing, bloodstream, sensitivity and intelligence, and is growing a brain and a nervous system. It is an organic and integral being. And of course it is not a living being in the middle of dead, empty space. It is, we can say, an endocrine gland of the living organism of the solar system which, seen spiritually, is a great entity with the sun as its living heart organ. Then we comprehend that all the planets are comparable to the endocrine glands of the body. And here is one of them gone badly wrong—dark, rigid, freezing up, hardening, growing brutalised, because its rightful steward has gone mad with greed and fear.

Remember that your body is a microcosm reflecting the macrocosm and that the secrets of the universe are to be read in its evolution. The Greeks carved above the great portal of the temple at Delphi: "Man, know thyself and thou shalt know the universe." That statement is more significant for us today, since we have virtually lost knowledge of the spiritual world and are now in process of recovering it. We are realising that humanity is not an accident of chance natural selection but part of the grand design. In other words, let us realise that the whole of nature is an amazing work of art. Behind it is the divine consciousness. Be aware that a great ocean of life and intelligence continually pours out of the divine source, and that within this ocean of Being there are strands of intelligence—facets of the Thought of God—that we call the angels.

This world of living Ideas has been externalised, expressed into visible form. The marvellous flowers we see, the trees, clouds, mountains, our own bodies, are the expression—the pressing out—of living, creative Ideas. And from that we come to the concept that the human being, the ensouled body, is the primal archetype, the primal Idea of God. It is a glorious notion. Behind, beyond, above all, stands the great archetype, the goal towards which all of us are working. This is the complete reversal of the notion that we are merely the product of chance natural selection. The first thing in creation was God's archetype of humanity, but it was the last to appear in physical form—hence the thought that we must have grown out of the monkeys. Humanity was the last to come because we are the final work of art. The whole of nature in its complexity had to develop first, in order to create a setting in which this great experiment could take place. It implies the realising of the archetype, like unto God, as a being who has achieved freedom and free will and therefore can become a conscious co-creator within the world of nature.

34

It is a terrific plan, a most exciting drama—the greatest saga in the whole of evolution. And this tiny and beautiful planet has been chosen as the setting for this work of art, this adventure in creating the co-creator. Just think how it will be when we, as individual souls, realise our own archetype. What shall we be as artists, as athletes, as lovers, as creators, once we have fully manifested the invisible divine being we really are and are approaching with every incarnation?

Now think into nature as a work of art. We are able to do fine things in sculpture, in building, in painting. But consider the achievement of something like a flower, the artistry that is able to take form and then let it metamorphose and transform itself. We have hardly begun to do that yet—not, at any rate, in the more solid or plastic arts, though in music we can experience the flowing metamorphosis of form.

Taking this idea that the human body is the measure for all things, realise what we are doing in our arts. Artists can do virtually nothing but externalise themselves, because everything is contained within the body. Therefore, to summarise briefly, we may feel that architecture, that basic art, inevitably grows out of the fact of the human skeleton. We experience the structure of ourselves and externalise this temple into the outer temple. The harmonics of the body are expressed in architectural form. You can sense how classical and Renaissance architecture, basically involving pillar and lintel, gives a structure which reflects the two legs and the pelvis, all rooted in gravity. The great Gothic architecture is in a sense a metamorphosis of the whole rib cage, lifted out of gravity—for remember, this body is the perfect balance of levity and gravity; that is why it is so wonderful. The human leg is given over entirely to the world of gravity, pointing right down to the centre of the Earth. The lifted spine and the poised head make a Grail chalice open to the inpouring powers of the spirit. The human arm is not an organ for perambulation as with the ape, but is lifted completely into the levity field and can therefore gesture, act, play the Kreuzer Sonata, express soul and serve the spirit. Gothic architecture, achieving a fantastic piece of engineering, puts all its emphasis on the soaring lift into levity, appearing to achieve weightlessness and the dematerialisation of stone. Thus to enter a Gothic cathedral is a profoundly spiritual experience.

The dome in Renaissance architecture is a direct metamorphosis of the human head, the thinking organ. This can be felt in St. Paul's Cathedral in London. We also sense that the great drum with its huge pillars is the rib cage metamorphosed. Then the Baroque style—the wonderful architecture of south Germany and Austria—shows a dissolving of the physical dome or ceiling and a breaking through into the heaven world so that, moving into the church, you look upwards and straight through into all the terraces of heaven. And there is the cross or some being in apotheosis, disappearing into the gold of heaven at a vast height. The whole of architecture is an externalisation of the human temple, and where humankind is still known as the measure of all things, we can find ourselves in the harmonics of the great buildings.

What, then, of sculpture? Here is a clue. Realise that, to some degree, sculpture can be an expression of the etheric body of humankind. It would seem that the great Greek sculptors were not working from models but from a true experience of their own etheric body, which is the basic structure of vital forces holding together the particles forming the visible body. That is why these great sculptures are so profoundly exciting.

Then in painting we move on to a soul or 'astral' level, where the heart and the emotions are externalised and it is possible to experience living colour. Let us realise that nothing we see in the physical world is without its spiritual counterpart. Therefore on a certain plane exists the ocean of living yellow that makes up spring, while the green of the grass and leaves is an expression in physical matter of sheer life. There is an ocean of colour invisible to the physical eyes but apparent to the artistic and inner consciousness. We are really taking hold of the life of the spiritual world as we contact living colour as a functional force in the dynamic universe.

Then entering the world of poetry we move over into the realm of thought and imagination. Handling the creative word is again another step in freedom. And beyond that we move into the world of spirit which is music. There is a book by Cyril Scott called *Music: Its Secret Influence through the Ages*, in which he has presented the thesis that composers do not reflect their period; rather, they create the following period. Handel comes to this country and composes for an England that has lost religion. He plays England back into religion. That wonderful moment when George II rises to the Hallelujah Chorus with tears in his eyes is really a turning point in history, a transforming of the English consciousness through music. And then comes Beethoven, composing in an age totally devoid of compassion. He plays compassion into the human spirit and in effect launches psychology. The reason why Beethoven mattered so much to the 19th century is that there was so much psychological repression at that time.

Cyril Scott carries his thesis through the centuries. We see that Delius, Scriabin and César Franck are for the first time opening to the elemental world of nature—a contact upon which the Findhorn Foundation has been built. In our own age there needs to be a smashing up of old thought forms, to prepare for what is coming next. In achieving this, sheer noise is a significant factor!

What, then, is coming next as we pass into the new age? Humanity is the brain and nervous system of a living planet. The whole of humanity is a living organism and each of us is a cell of that organism. Realise that that thought was not possible until this generation. You are a part of the life—the brain—of Gaia, the goddess of Earth. Remember this: all this new age stuff is not somebody's carefully thought-out plan for improving society—something that has happened often enough in the last centuries. What is happening now is a response to a force flooding into the planet. Force-fields of light and spiritual power are entering the dying existence of Earth and lifting the vibratory rate. Naturally, those particles of humanity which are attuned will lift into higher consciousness, and those not attuned will be repelled by these force-fields. They will find that they cannot live surrounded by this higher frequency, and will be thrown out. This all indicates that we are taking part in a tremendous process of redemption of the planet.

I call one of my books *Operation Redemption* to imply that this is something happening now, in our time. There never was such a generation in which to be alive, because we stand on the threshold of the Aquarian Age and, although it is a longish process, the actual turning point is coming in the next 15 years. You young people are carrying the brunt of the whole thing. Dare I say I congratulate you on having incarnated at this moment, by choice? You were shown the destiny you were taking on and given the chance to back out—and you didn't. Thank you. Neither did I. We've all come in on it, and it is tremendous. This is the greatest saga in the whole of human history and we are taking part in it.

Here I offer a passage from 'the Tibetan', that great master who wrote through Alice Bailey:

*Aquarius is a living sign, and an emotional sign. It will stimulate the astral bodies of men to new coherency, into a brotherhood of humanity, which will ignore all racial and national differences, and will carry the life of men forward into synthesis and unity. This means a tide of unifying life of such power that one cannot now*

*envisage it, but which in a thousand years will have welded all
mankind to a perfect brotherhood. Its emotional effect will be to
purify the astral bodies of men so that the material world ceases to
hold such potent allure. There will then emerge a creativity of such
wondrous dimensions that the world will stand amazed. Nothing like
it will have been seen before. A creative planning for human well-
being, and political expression implementing that planning, will
demonstrate in every country. A creative thinking will be apparent,
which will express itself in writing and poetry. Creative imagining
will produce new art, new colours, new architecture and a new
culture. A creative responsiveness to the music of the spheres will
bring forth new music. The creative art of today will be to this new
creative art what a child's building in wooden blocks is to great
cathedrals such as Durham or Milan.*

This is the prospect for us, and it is grand. The breakthrough is happening. I throw at you one little quotation from an enchanting book
called *The Mystics Come to Harley Street*, a collection of statements
about peak experiences by people who have made the breakthrough
into wider consciousness:

*In a moment, range upon range of new thought showed itself in stag-
gering immensity, accompanied by a sense of conviction, almost like
a voice in its compelling reassurance that all was real and all was
truth. And I was left with a breathtaking sense of the limitless power
and certainty of God, the tranquillity which can only be described as
'the peace that passes all understanding'. I was left with a new sense
of certainty that all things work out together for good.*

I have said that we are taking part in the greatest drama of the whole
of history. Basically it is the story of the fall and redemption of
humankind. We are droplets of divinity who belong to another world
and have undergone the Fall into the darkness of Earth, which at times
seems like hell. We now have the excitement of being at that real turning point when the old bottles are being smashed to make ready for the
outpouring of the new Aquarian wine. We are making ourselves into a
new bottle—and a fine bottle is the Findhorn Foundation!

Now here is a poem written by a young Irishman called Tim
Jackson. When I was lecturing in Ireland, his mother—a friend of
mine—asked me what I thought of it. Well, I took it and used it in my

lecture, with the young poet sitting in the front row. It is called *Parousia*, a Greek word meaning 'the presence beyond' or 'the presence behind', which touches the great fact of the presence of the Christ Being everywhere, in our own hearts and in all nature.

*We are falling yet*
*And the notes still spill into our minds,*
*Gather and hold in brief recreation*
*Of that first awful stillness*
*That seeded the stars into our cosmos.*

*Feebly we feel into the recesses*
*After the receding light of the Lost Glory of Man*
*When he sang with the morning stars*
*At the dawn of time.*

*Yet there is hope for a new synthesis,*
*Drawing together the strands of creation*
*Converging*
*Under the banner of Christ.*
*It is happening, quietly, inevitably,*
*Trickling into all corners*
*Like the rising tide.*

*Many are too heavy to lift into the new perception*
*Drowned in the density of their many necessities,*
*Trapped in the tensions of life's trivia.*
*Yet some, even now*
*Hear the whisper and slap of running water*
*And work and work*
*Knowing that soon their life will lift from the inertia of history*
*And they will sail, singing, with the storm of His Coming.*

# Chapter Three
# The Vision of Wholeness

*Onearth Conference, October 1976*
*'The World Crisis and the Wholeness of Life'*

Dear friends, may I first express my profound delight at speaking in this Universal Hall. I think here is a real link with Attingham*, for the Findhorn Foundation is becoming one of the great centres of adult education. There is no doubt that, during the great quarter of a century that Attingham was going, it was a unique place and a leader in certain ways. Looking back, one can see that those first courses on spiritual themes were really making history. I had the opportunity in those post-war years of putting on weekend courses on every kind of theme in order to fire people's imagination and enthusiasm.

During the 50s and 60s I began to experiment with the spiritual world view and discovered that courses like 'The Expansion of Consciousness', 'The Adventure of Dying', 'The Quest for the Grail in our Time' or 'Frontiers of Reality' packed the house. Here was a phenomenon in the field of adult education. We had discovered an unmet demand: the quest for the real meaning of life through a spiritual world-view. I think we are now establishing its place in British adult education. Such a gathering as this conference is obviously on the highest level of adult education for the future. Therefore, it is a great personal delight to be part of this bridging operation of lecturing in this hall now.

I begin my theme by giving you Gerard Manley Hopkins' great sonnet, *God's Grandeur*. This shows us how human beings have polluted the planet and that the true answer lies in the vision of wholeness.

*From 1947-71 Sir George was principal of the Shropshire Adult College in Attingham Park, an 18th century mansion used as a cultural centre open to everyone and running short residential courses.

There are several communications received from high spiritual sources which imply essentially that so long as we go on treating the planet as a tiny, isolated speck of dead mineral twirling in a vast mechanical universe, we can never solve the planetary problems we have created. Human self-sufficiency alone is not enough. If, however, we can wake up to our relationship to the wholeness of life and the fact that the universe is a vast living organism shot through and through with creative being, and if we can then channel and cooperate with the energies and forces from that living universe, there is nothing that cannot be solved, even to the possibility of molecular change which could de-pollute the planet. This is the factor that ordinary ecology, economics and science in their materialism wholly ignore as so much airy thinking. And here is the great paradox: that our apparently airy thinking is in fact the perfectly practical key without which the great problems will not be solved. Here is the answer, put poetically:

*The world is charged with the grandeur of God.*
*It will flame out, like shining from shook foil;*
*It gathers to a greatness like the ooze of oil*
*Crushed. Why do men then now not reck his rod?*
*Generations have trod, have trod, have trod;*
*And all is seared with trade; bleared smeared with toil*
*And wears man's smudge and shares man's smell; the soil*
*Is bare now, nor can foot feel, being shod.*

*And for all this, nature is never spent;*
*There lives the dearest freshness deep down things;*
*And though the last light off the black West went*
*Oh, morning, at the brown brink eastwards, springs*
*Because the Holy Ghost over the bent*
*World broods with warm breast and with ah! bright wings.*

The Earth is overlighted by the power of the Cosmic Christ and of the living Hierarchy, who are deeply concerned with the future of the planet. This is the implication of the Oneness thinking. We are now experiencing the greatest revolution in the intellectual climate of human thought: we are discovering that this planet is not just a tiny, unimportant speck in the universe, nor are we the only civilisation. This Earth is of paramount importance as a channelling point through which spiritual being on all levels can flow and evolve. Humanity is to be seen as a great experiment of God going through the illusion of separation from the divine Oneness and evolving self-consciousness to achieve conscious reintegration with the divine will, in free creativity, as co-creator and companion of God. Of course, we know that the whole field of humankind is vastly bigger than the four billion we see embodied upon this planet, for a great number of souls are living between incarnations, and many, many other beings have had to pass through this focal point at some stage or other. Therefore Earth in its beauty is of immeasurable importance in the whole universal pattern. The extraordinary paradox is that in our arrogance, seeing ourselves merely as an accident in evolution, we have felt free to exploit the planet and even to destroy life upon it; while in the new humility that comes as we grasp the vision of wholeness we realise that humanity has a divine purpose in the universe.

As we grasp this vision, we take upon our shoulders once more the immeasurably important task of becoming the bridging point of consciousness in touch with the worlds of spirit. For humankind is the point where evolution has become conscious of itself, integrally part of the whole of nature, a pulse of the eternal mind, no less. Each of us is that point within nature where higher worlds can enter and make contact.

The bridge is eternally present, for there is no other time but this immediate moment, 'the intersection point of the timeless with time'. In this moment life is perpetually nascent, day always dawning. We see the prospect of a life in which we can move in joyous dance from instant to instant. This applies to any and every activity, for we are learning in each moment to become creative out of our own still centre. Limitless Love and Truth lives and exists in this centre within each of us. And in this centre, united with the dance of the immediate moment, we are one with the whole.

We live in an age when we are being forced to grow up, when, as has been well demonstrated within the Findhorn Foundation, outward guidance is being withdrawn so that we are compelled to rely upon our own inner guidance. But we are also moving into an age of which Christ himself has said, "Behold, I make all things new." What is going to be the use of our old brain tracks and habit patterns in such an age? Clearly this brings us to the major educational challenge with which centres like the Findhorn Foundation must experiment. Our task in education is not to build structures of knowledge as such, thereby fixing people in certain habits of belief, but rather somehow to train them so that they can abandon old paradigms and enter into the greatest adventure, which is to set forth on a journey into wholeness.

We are in touch with the eternal worlds, and the light can be given to us in relation to the demands of the immediate moment. In other words, this is a *new* creativity and we are going to be faced constantly with situations for which we have absolutely no human precedent: situations for which none of the old brain tracks are going to be any use. A powerful image here would be of a panther with all its wonderful instincts let loose in the traffic of Piccadilly at rush hour. All the glory of its animal instincts would be perfectly useless and the beast would panic. Only a creature who in a comparable situation could inhibit instant reaction, maintain poise, do nothing and listen to get the inspiration from the higher self for a course of action never before followed could rightly enter this age of change. And humankind is the creature which has this capacity. In Shakespeare's words:

> *They that have power to hurt and will do none,*
> *That do not do the thing they most do show,*
> *Who moving others, are themselves as stone,*
> *Unmoved, cold, and to temptation slow,*
> *They rightly do inherit Heaven's graces,*
> *And husband nature's riches from expence,*
> *They are the Lords and owners of their faces,*
> *Others but stewards of their excellence....*

This ability involves a recognition that our higher self, united with the oneness of things and filled with the Christ impulse and the light, has the overall picture and is guiding our destiny. We, as conscious personality, are moving through the maze, even lost in it, but the higher self looks down and can guide us out. This calls for the creative use of imagination—a sensing of how our higher self would react—and then having the courage to act, literally with the higher self. It is not for nothing that the British are the greatest race of amateur actors: it is ingrained in our bones. But we needn't go in for acting clubs or Shakespeare societies: rather, we can see that we are all acting a part in the truest sense, into our higher self, and that in this immediate moment—in every single situation—we can will meaning creatively into our reaction and choose the course which leads to greater wholeness.

So we move into the new, guided by this higher reality. Such a course of action would be impossible unless we grasp the reality of the higher worlds. Therefore what centres like the Findhorn Foundation should be doing educationally is teaching the basic techniques by which we can understand how the wisdom tradition floods through all human expression. Behind that tradition is the wisdom of the Hierarchy and the great mystery centres which exist on the higher plane and are now once more breaking through into human consciousness. In the great operation for the redemption of the planet, humanity can and must cooperate. Operation Redemption has indeed been launched. This is the logical conclusion that follows from our vision of wholeness. And this is the great excitement of our time.

Humanity had to undergo the Fall, moving out of innocence through experience, entering deep into the morass of the physical and sensual before beginning to move out again on the ascent which Blake calls Imagination—not back to Eden garden, but on to the New Jerusalem which we are taking part in creating. We are now at this immensely exciting point when it becomes possible to make the breakthrough. This is the logical result of the human intellect developing itself so acutely that it first shows physical matter to be energy, then discovers that energy is also alive and that therefore this same universe of energy is a universe of thought, of intelligence, of creative being. In this way the passage through intellectual self-consciousness quite naturally leads the advanced thinking of the physicists to identify with the mystic mind.

We see that in tackling our problems the great challenge to ecologists, scientists and politicians is to bring the mystics into the picture. Ecology is beginning to study how life works as an immense whole, but meantime we are destroying life upon the planet. How then can we comprehend the concept of wholeness? Who can think wholeness? Not the ecologist, not the scientist, emphatically not the technologist. Only the adepts or initiates can in consciousness expand their understanding and, through a direct blending with Universal Mind, speak from the whole, or allow the whole to speak through them. Only they can assess the effects on the planet of certain courses of action, and only they can really be the touchstone to say what technological humankind may or may not safely and rightly do to the whole. We had an example of this when Wellesley Tudor Pole and other seers sent long cables to the President of the United States concerning the first high-level nuclear explosions, urging him to realise that not only would this allow dangerous rays down to the surface of the Earth by rending the etheric envelope of the planet, but that it would also allow the darkest and most dangerous of the spiritual beings, the Azuras, to enter into human life and to attack the soul and spirit. But of course that can mean nothing to a materialistic mind with no notion of the spiritual nature of the universe. However, the time may come when ecology, conservation and politics can begin to bring the adepts and mystics into consultation.

The great problem now is that we should save the life upon this planet by learning to share the Earth's goods. Three-quarters of the Earth is dying of hunger, largely because we in the West haven't found out how to do this. Our ordinary efforts are still based upon the profit motive, so how can we share and not make a loss? And a loss is what we must not make, because we have to make money. So we are completely stymied! How do we even give away the surplus? Who is to tell us how to share? So we come to the tremendous concept that the Hierarchy—the Masters, the great adepts, human beings who have not needed to incarnate for many centuries—have been overlighting and working invisibly in human consciousness. One of the greatest of them overlights this very place. It appears that many of these Masters have resolved to re-enter human life either through physical birth or by using a resurrection body which they can take on and reject at will. They will appear as people whose vision is so wide that they will carry absolute conviction in what they say, bringing understanding as to how we can solve our problems in the light of the vision of wholeness. They will bring an impulse by which we shall see how to share. Consider the impact of such people as Schweitzer and Schumacher. These were not Masters, but they were great spirits of such a scale that their lives and work have spread light and understanding. Everyone has heard Schumacher's phrase 'small is beautiful'. New vision has been awakened by such people.

If the 'externalisation of the Hierarchy' actually takes place as foretold, then a group of very exalted beings will move among us as humans, bringing an impulse to goodwill and non-violence. And this, of course, will be in preparation for the Second Coming, whatever form that event is going to take. It does not matter what name you call the Great Being of all Light—Limitless Love and Truth, the Christos, the Maitreya, the Imam Mahdi, Krishna, the Messiah—the fact is that the Lord of Light now overlights the entire planet and is present in all life everywhere. This is the ultimate vision of wholeness. He entered as the Christ 2000 years ago, but found humanity unprepared to receive the real message of wholeness and oneness at that time. Nevertheless he launched the impulse. His descent was the most important compliment that could be paid to a tiny planet. As Alice Meynell writes in her poem *Christ in the Universe*, "Our wayside planet bears as chief treasure one forsaken grave." Once he went through human life and human death—the only time a God has done that. Now this same exalted Being overlights the whole of humanity, whatever race or creed. The wholeness and light are one. He has said: "I am the resurrection and the life." He didn't say: "I am resurrected and alive," but "I *am* the life." He is the Lord of all Light, the Solar Logos, embodied in the etheric body of the Earth and therefore present within every nuclear centre, within every cell, form and flower and every human heart.

It has been said that in the closing years of this century more and more people will go through the same experience as Paul on the road to Damascus. They will be initiated by the blinding light and will know that the Christ is alive. He will more and more frequently appear at critical moments of great tension. This is a mystery about which there are many tales—of the one who turns up unexpectedly and is able to spread goodwill in a terrible situation. Here I recommend a book, *Not Too Narrow, Not Too Deep* by Richard Sale (Pilgrim Book Services), a short and brilliant novel which depicts what is coming to change people's lives.

The coming of the Avatar or Saviour is being brought about through the urgency of this time of distress. We are to expect events, pressures, happenings, changes which will indicate that this Being is present and the Masters are among us once more. We must watch and see what the next years will bring, for human consciousness moves towards the Cosmic Sense and we are that point within nature which can receive it.

Here is a passage from Edward Carpenter in which the Cosmic Sense is speaking. This is quoted in Bucke's great book *Cosmic Consciousness*. Of course, the wording identifies the Living Christ.

*There is no peace, except where I am, saith the Lord,*
*I alone remain, I do not change.*
*As space spreads everywhere, and all things move and change*
   *within it,*
*but it moves not, nor it changes,*
*So I am the space within the soul,*
*of which the space without is but the similitude or mental image.*
*Comest thou to inhabit me, thou hast entrance to all life.*
*Death shall no longer divide thee from those thou lovest.*
*I am the Sun that shines upon all creatures from within.*
*Gazest thou upon me, thou shalt be filled with joy eternal.*
*Be not deceived; soon this outer world shall drop off—*

*thou shalt slough it away as a man sloughs his mortal body.*
*Learn even now to spread thy wings in that other world,*
*to swim in the ocean, my child, of Me and My Love.*
*Ah, have I not taught thee by the semblances of this outer world,*
*by its alienations, and deaths, and mortal sufferings,*
*all for this—for joy, ah, joy unutterable.*

And finally, from the book *The Shining Brother* by Lawrence Temple (Gateway Books), here is one of the messages from the High Source, communicated by St Francis to the author, who in a previous incarnation was Brother Lawrence of Assisi. This assuredly speaks to us all about what is happening in our time.

*The time has come when the mysteries of the age shall be revealed to all who desire light upon their path, that they may approach the centre of all Power and of Life. For a new spirit is within the world and man throws off his leading strings, and will no longer follow blindly the blind leaders. He will accept instruction only from those who can perceive the invisible and hear the unspoken word, who are filled with the spirit and who speak with inner knowledge and have escaped from the bondage of creeds and the inherited beliefs of past generations. For the soul of man requires freedom for the growth of the new age and strength to carry the burden of greater responsibilities. Therefore upon many will be poured forth the gifts of the spirit, that light may penetrate the darkness and humanity be reborn nearer to the Divine Image. This is a Day of Days, when many forces meet and much is shattered in the impact: yet in the Infinite Mind is the supreme thought, the creative urge towards perfection, and we who dwell in the eternal harmony are at one with these vast waves of power. And all our being is given to this invincible direction of the thought forms of God. For his children work each in their degree, and the power is transformed by the creative activity of his ministers, for there is no break in the chain between the least and the greatest. The creative power floweth through all, and each is a partaker in the divine plan and giveth that which he hath to the Universal Heritage.*

# Chapter Four
# Let There Be Light

*Onearth Conference, October 1980*
*'Ecology of Light: A Gathering of Earth's Stories'*

The Book of Genesis begins with the words: "In the beginning God created Heaven and Earth...." A very interesting variant on that theme is found in the Essene Book of Creation, the book of Moses. Listen to the opening words: "Without beginning, the Law creates life and thought."

What a wonderful concept, that without beginning the Law creates life and thought. There is a continuous process of inpouring of new life to counter deadening entropy. Moses discovered the one ultimate Law which controls all other laws and saw that all our human sufferings arise through deviation from that Law. He taught the Essenes to conceive of the Oceans of Life, Thought, Will and Love. Let us stretch our minds to grasp this vast continuum of life, love and thought, which is the first manifestation of God—an ocean of archetypal Ideas.

According to the first chapter of Genesis, God made the plants, birds and fishes each 'after their kind', and then he created the human being, male and female, 'after his own image': androgynous. Then at the beginning of the second chapter it says that there were no plants on Earth because it had not yet rained. There comes a second creation: the animals, the fishes, the plants, Adam and then Eve taken from Adam's fifth rib. The first creation must be seen as the creation of archetypal Ideas—the group ego, so to speak, of each plant and animal —which then have to be realised in physical creation. The archetypal Ideas pour themselves into reflection in physical form, and therefore within every plant, tree and animal is the living being. The outer physical form is but the sheath for spirit to dip down into the field of gravity.

In our imagination we have conceived the great Oneness of being and of life. This is the primal condition: air and fire, warmth and light, pouring in from the far periphery. Then come water and earth working from the gravity centre of the planet. In our imagination let us conceive this polarity of gravity working from the centre of the Earth upwards, and the counter-pole, levity, operating from the far periphery. Note this remarkable fact, that human thinking in these last three centuries since the time of Newton has concerned itself solely with the gravity pole, the drag towards the centre of a body. We have based our interpretation of the universe on this centripetal pull, and the interrelationship of heavenly bodies has been calculated on the basis of the balance of gravity pulls keeping things in relation in a vast empty space. However, the whole of nature and life is based on polarities, as is stated in the principles of the Hermetic Wisdom, and we must recover the concept of the primal polarity: levity working from the periphery and gravity working from the centre, poised and meeting on the surface of the globe.

What is being recovered in our time is the concept of 'ethereal space'. The opposite of gravity is not just something very light as opposed to the very heavy, but something absolutely and qualitatively different. We have to conceive of a vast realm of expanding, buoyant, uplifting forces which pervade the world: the anti-gravity counter-pull of the great circumference. First comes the life pole of warmth and light. The death pole, the 'grave' of gravity, derives from that. The human being is the point where the meeting of these two realms—gravity and levity—is achieved in perfection. Here is the organism which is given over in its lower limbs wholly to gravity, with legs directed right down towards the centre of the Earth. The head poised upon the upright spine is open in its crown chakra like a chalice. The animal with its horizontal spine carries a head which is still held by the gravity forces and which has been turned into a kind of tool. Think of the beaks of birds or the teeth of animals or the amazing and sensitive trunk of the elephant; then think of the human face, an organ which can really express soul through the smile, something no animal can do. Our beloved dog can grin, but we must admit it is not capable of a smile in the human sense, where the soul shines out of the face. And think of human arms, which are capable of handling tools for art or crafts, capable of dance, of acting, of expressing emotion and soul quality. The human being is poised between the realm of Earth and that of Heaven and is the meeting point of all divine energies. And in thought we are directly united with the Ocean of Thought. The human brain weighs 22 ounces, but since it floats in liquid, by displacement it in effect weighs only two ounces. It is therefore lifted out of gravity, and the human head, in the midst of the greatest action, is poised and still in control—open, like a chalice, to the thought of the cosmos. So the human being is truly a bridging point between the two worlds.

The recovery of this knowledge of ethereal space is of the greatest importance and marks a revolution in human thinking, opening the possibility for a leap in human consciousness. We are weighted down by centuries of matter- and sense-bound thinking and we need to take a leap in consciousness in order to expand into our true home; to realise that space is not empty but is the field of an absolute condition of life, thought and being, which is eternal and outside time. We find 'eternity' such a difficult concept because we are still bedevilled by the mediaeval concept of either 'eternal damnation' if we have behaved badly, or—almost as bad—eternally sitting upon a cloud playing a harp if we have behaved well. This use of the word 'eternal' implies 'to the end of time' and thus is essentially a time-ridden concept. We must understand eternity as the condition outside time. We touch it in meditation; at night we all enter it in sleep; and we shall of course enter it after death.

The great myth of the human soul is the descent of spirit into form, to sojourn in time and matter, to work within the realm of gravity and then be released again, having matured in experience. Such inbreathing and outbreathing is the essential pattern of nature. Throughout the living world we see the workings of the spirit through metamorphosis of form. This suggests an exciting way of looking at nature which combines a scientific approach with artistic and imaginative vision.

Let us start with the concept of the plant as first revealed by Goethe in his discovery of its metamorphosis. Goethe was profoundly disturbed and irritated by the conventional scientific thinking of his time, which was analysing and dissecting plants and putting them in categories under the inspiration of Linnaeus. He knew that this approach was not touching the real wonder and mystery of life. What is the plant doing? The clue lies in the realisation that the plant is all leaf, in the sense that the leaf organ can transform itself in all directions, so that every part of the plant is a metamorphosis of leaf. Look at the plant pushing its roots down into the earth. As it grows, it begins to unfold leaves. Use your imaginative vision and notice that in two or three moves our plant has achieved what we can recognise as the greatest splendour of its leaf form. Here is a very simple and important point: how is it that we know a leaf has achieved what it was trying to do? Something in our minds has the ability to recognise the reality of the archetype pouring itself in-

50

to visible form in the plant; its 'idea' is fulfilled. By looking imaginatively into the growing plant, we see how leaf transmutes into sepals,
grouped as if the leaves were spinning round the stalk. And then the
miracle happens: petals appear—coloured; petal is leaf metamorphosed.

When we learn to look into the plant with imaginative vision and
close observation, so that we move with changing nature, we shall suddenly get the clue. The tulip, for instance, will throw out its splendid
leaves, long stalk and crimson petals, but half an inch down it will often
throw out an extra petal or 'sport'. This you will observe is half green
leaf and half red petal, to the artistic eye absolute proof that the plant
has lifted right up into an ethereal plane and transformed itself into
colour, light and scent. Now, for further proof, look into the rose. You
will find that the outer petal has a tiny nick in the top and that in the
next one further in that nick has hardened into a little cyst which, in a
later petal nearer the centre, will have turned into something of a rib.
Then you will find a tiny bit of yellowing towards pollen, after which
the outer flanges fall away and the complete pollen organ will be left. So
stamen is petal metamorphosed, petal is leaf metamorphosed.

What Goethe realised and Rudolf Steiner developed is this artistic/
scientific way of looking. Goethe called it 'exact sensorial imagination',
for if you can really take that plant and think step by step through the
expansion of its leaves, through transformation into petal, expansion
into fruit and finally contraction back into seed, you can experience the
whole cycle and see the plant as a being in continuous flowing movement. Each plant begins to reveal its secret. It begins, in a sense, to
speak to you. What then is the seed? The whole new plant is not contained in the seed. The seed is chaoticised matter, total formlessness.
The plant dies and you throw it upon the compost heap and it rots
down into humus, the matrix for all life. But the seed remains and,
given the conditions of warmth and moisture, the living archetypal
Idea from the field of light begins to pour itself once again into the
fructifying seed.

Grasp this thought: the Earth does not create form; the Earth forces
destroy form. The Earth is the mother—the womb—of course, but life
is fructified from the heavenly source. The Earth is the point where
spiritual ideas can pour into form. Through the cycle of growth and
decay, the Idea of the plant—the elemental being of the group ego—is
released again into that realm of light and width and movement. It
passes through restriction and release, systole and diastole, breathing
in and breathing out.

Goethe's vision can be further understood through the butterfly. Think of the caterpillar—a splendid fellow of black and yellow, crawling along with such pride. Then comes the moment when it hangs itself up and spins a cocoon about itself. Inside the pupa the caterpillar disintegrates and turns to mere sludge. Unable to see ahead, what disappointment it must feel remembering its splendid days as a caterpillar! And then, miracle upon miracle, the wing cells begin to form *from the outside inwards* into a pattern of wings. The Idea of a butterfly works down into the formless sludge. Finally, the moment comes when it can break out and at once is capable of fluttering into the sunlight with that glitter of blue-gold on its wings. This gold dust on the butterfly's wings is the nearest thing we can conceive to living sunlight.

The stages of metamorphosis in the butterfly closely parallel those in the plant. Thus we may truly see butterfly as flower animated or flower as butterfly caught down into matter. No wonder the two seem so closely linked. Metamorphosis would seem to be working all the time throughout nature, perpetually lifting, transforming, transmuting back to the more refined. Consider the great clouds, for instance. The nimbus clouds are given over to the world of gravity, depositing rain upon us. Above those are the great cumulus clouds in which air is rising at 15 feet per second so that, if you are in a glider and are caught up in them, you fall upwards and are spewed out of the top. Watch them as they go through their cycle. They rise with enormous energy and almost architectural majesty; then comes a stage when they reach an obvious ceiling and begin to widen out into a great anvil shape, and the energy goes from them. They become high stratus, which then is blown away on the wind like cotton wool.

See and really experience this rising energy in the cumulus clouds, and realise that it is not adequately accounted for by the mere explanation that hot air rises. With our artistic and spiritual vision we must see that the clouds represent matter moving out into the realm of levity; they are given over to the pull that goes to the far periphery; gravity/levity, the primary polarity, is at work within them. And beyond the cumulus clouds lies the glory of the delicate forms of the high cirrus clouds. In these we see that in the final metamorphosis, water vapour does not simply fall again as rain, but is actually dematerialised into etheric space to re-form as dew and snow. Think of the miraculous beauty of form in snowflakes and the wonder of fresh dew on the grass, and conceive that this is absolute virgin matter dropped out of the ethereal realm of spirit into the physical.

We are struggling to recover an understanding of this etheric pole to which our consciousness belongs. This theme is developed by George Adams, the great anthroposophical writer, and by Rudolf Steiner in the book *Man as Symphony of the Creative Word*. It is of paramount importance to us now to realise that the Newtonian world picture is only a partial truth. It has analysed one aspect of the universe, the pull to the centre, but it has left out the primary polarity. The most important book on this theme is *Man or Matter*, by Dr Ernst Lehrs, which presents this primary polarity of gravity and levity as seen by the Goethean world view. As we sensed when considering the Book of Genesis, the death pole—gravity, the grave—is secondary to the light/life pole of levity. The human race is the meeting point between the two. There is nothing essentially stopping the human mind from uniting with the Thought Field and expanding into the universal Ocean of Mind. We must have the courage to take the step into widening consciousness. This is well expressed in a sonnet by John Charles Earle called *Bodily Extension:*

*The body is not bounded by its skin.*
*Its effluence, like a gentle cloud of scent,*
*Is wide into the air diffused, and blent*
*With elements unseen, its way doth win*
*To ether frontiers, where take origin*
*Far subtler systems, nobler regions meant*
*To be the area and the instrument*
*Of operations ever to begin*
*Anew and never end. Thus every man*
*Wears as his robe the garment of the sky,*
*So close his union with the cosmic plan,*
*So perfectly he pierces low and high,*
*Reaching as far in space as creature can*
*And co-extending with immensity.*

This is our inner space exploration, the counterpart to our physical exploration of space. The shooting of rockets round the moon, however exciting and important, is still based on the gravity pole. We are concerned with the levity pole and the exploration of ethereal space, the gateway to which is our own consciousness. When we look at nature's forms with imaginative observation, so that they speak to us of how levity and gravity interplay in living harmony, then we begin this exploration. Once we cross that frontier there will be no end to adult education! As Lessing wrote: "Is not the whole of Eternity mine?"

"Thus every man wears as his robe the garment of the sky...." This is the significance of the new age. The human race is approaching the frontier when we will be able to take such a step and enter the ethereal world. For metamorphosis applies not only to plants and animals, but to the whole of life of which we are a part, including the human soul. Goethe was once asked if he could explain the secret of life. He replied: "You want to know the secret of life? That which the plant does unconsciously, do consciously. That is all." In other words, we are called on to go through these stages within the soul; to realise that we also are rooted down into the darkness of the Earth, as is a tree, but that one part of us reaches upwards, and our task is to metamorphose the soul.

Now widen that thought into the whole of society, for everything is organism within organism. A social body, a town or a country—all are living organisms and every organism has its angelic being. We need to recognise that we are working with the angelic world and that for every human grouping there is a guardian angel. A community such as this has an angelic being and the folk-soul of a nation is a great archangelic being. Our society is going through chaotic times as a result of deviation from the One Law. Absolutely fundamental to renewal is the breakdown and death of the old outer form. Goethe has said: "Nature invented death that there might be more abundant life." In other words, the outer form—whether human, animal or plant—must die in order to release the imperishable spirit within it. There can be no death for the spirit, for it is life; but the form can be rejected when its task is done. Our society is poised on the threshold of changes which are to allow this ethereal, angelic world to flood in and take over Earth, and humankind is the conscious instrument for achieving this. In order for this momentous event to happen—and we may, if we will, call it the Second Coming—much that is dark has to be swept away. To quote Goethe again: "If you have not got this, this concept of death and becoming, you are but a dull guest in a dark world."

'Dying to become'—that is the secret. We know that for our inner being, our essence, there is no death. We are pure spirit, imperishable. Death is the process of discarding the outward sheath. In our death-ridden culture it is so important for us to realise that the manifestations of disorder, cruelty, violence, war and so forth are probably only a prelude to the great cleansing and the coming of the Light. We are taking part in this metamorphosis; we are being metamorphosed as a race, and we are to accept this cleansing process.

The first of all Earth's stories is that of the Light of Spirit descending into the imprisonment of Earth, in due course to be released again. All the myths and fairy tales remind us of this. Let me take one Earth story, the simplest of Grimm's Fairy Tales, which when analysed reveals the basic truth. There was once a princess who lived in her father's palace in the mountains (When did she live? When indeed did she not live?) and her cruel father drives her out to go down into the dark forest. She takes with her no luggage but three walnut shells: one containing a robe made of the light of the sun, another a robe made of the light of the stars and the third a robe made from the light of the moon. Losing her way in the night of the forest, she hides in a hollow oak. In the morning she is discovered by a huntsman of the region to which she has come, who asks her name and where she came from. But she has forgotten both; she simply cannot remember. So he takes her back to his lord's castle and there, since she can't even give her name, she is set to the meanest scullery work and only at the times of the festivals is she allowed to come out and dance, wearing one of her robes of light. On one of these occasions she meets the prince. They fall in love, are married, and he takes her back to the realm from which she has descended. And if they are not dead yet...well, they are living still.

It is interesting to note, incidentally, that opening and closing. The right opening is not just 'once upon a time' but that little comment to the effect: "Where did this happen? Where indeed did this not happen? When did it happen? Ah, when indeed did it not happen?" The implication, for those who have ears to hear, is that we are talking about something timeless. And instead of just saying at the end, "And they all lived happily ever after" an appropriate final comment is: "And if they are not dead yet...well, they are living still." We are talking about the eternal. The princess is the soul or self. She lives on the plane of light in a beautiful palace. Her apparently cruel father, God the Divine, pushes her out and she undergoes the Fall. She goes down to the forest, that eternal symbol in mythology for this difficult level of earthly life. There she hides herself in the hollow tree. What is this, other than the skull? The eternal being, wearing the garment of the sky, has shut itself down into this hollow skull and therefore forgets its name and whence it came. Is that not what all of us have done? Then she is taken by the huntsman of this Earth district back to the castle where, like the prodigal son, she is set to work on the lowest level of material substance. But during the festivals, those moments of the year when there is contact with the higher worlds, the soul is able to come out to dance, and there she meets the prince, who represents the higher self. The princess is the ego which has been pushed down into Earth life for the great training experience. In other myths and fairy stories the soul or personality is represented by, say, the younger son and the heroine is the higher self. The marriage of the personality to the higher self brings about redemption, so the soul can return to the higher plane. In our intellectual age, interpretation can help to bring the myths alive for us.

Now I give you a strange poem by Walt Whitman, called *Whispers of Heavenly Death*:

*Darest thou now O Soul*
*Walk out with me towards the unknown region,*
*Where neither ground is for the feet nor any path to follow?*

*No map there, nor guide,*
*Nor voice sounding, nor touch of human hand,*
*Nor face with blooming flesh, nor lips, nor eyes are in that land.*

*I know it not O Soul,*
*Nor dost thou, all is blank before us,*
*All waits undream'd of in that region, that inaccessible land.*

*Till when the ties loosen*
*All but the ties eternal, Time and Space,*
*Nor darkness, gravitation, sense, nor any bounds bounding us.*

*Then we burst forth, we float,*
*In Time and Space, O Soul, prepared for them,*
*Equal, equipped at last (O Joy, O fruit of all)*
    *them to fulfil O Soul.*

A remarkable statement indeed! The 'I' is talking to the soul. Darest thou, O friends, step out into the ethereal plane, knowing that it is not empty space but life, and that we, in mind, in thought, are part of life? We are free to step straight through, if we can overcome gravity and achieve sense-free thinking. We are rightly rooted in the world of gravity, but we are equally counter-rooted in the world of levity and the living spirit. Dare we take that step? If so, there is nothing stopping us in this path towards cosmic consciousness. The whole potential of humankind is infinite once that step can be taken. "Till when the ties loosen, nor darkness, gravitation, sense, nor any bounds bounding us, then we burst forth, we float in time and space...." Then comes a tremendous thought. Whitman, an initiate with cosmic consciousness, has the profound vision that time and space are not fulfilled until human consciousness—this strand of imprisoned divinity—expands into them. And that triumphant culmination he calls the 'Joy', the 'fruit of all'. Exploration of ethereal space in living thinking is our goal indeed. Perhaps this is the meaning of the great passage in Romans 8, which would be a fitting end to this talk:

*The Spirit of God joins with our spirit in testifying that we are God's children; and if children, then heirs. We are God's heirs and Christ's fellow-heirs if we share his sufferings now in order to share his splendour hereafter. For I reckon that the sufferings we now endure bear no comparison with the splendour, as yet unrevealed, which is in store for us. For the created universe waits with eager anticipation for God's sons to be revealed.*

# Chapter Five
# The Dissolution of Barriers

*'European Spiritual Community' Conference, October 1976*

The more we think about it, the more it seems that we must approach all our problems in the light of the emerging spiritual world view, which is the most notable phenomenon in the intellectual climate of our age. In the heart of a great materialistic culture, this ever-widening vision rises into consciousness and constantly increases in certainty.

We have been given a tremendous task of receiving the gift of free will and growing into free moral beings who can from our own inner decision reunite with the will of God. In order that we might become free beings, we had to go through the terrible and wonderful experience of separation in developing selfhood. Thus, through the ages we have developed intellectual consciousness and with it acute self-knowledge, selfhood and egoism. The price we have had to pay for the development of our intellect is the atrophying of those organs of perception which enabled us to know our relation to the whole and to know the reality of the inner, invisible, spiritual worlds of being.

The ancient Greeks could see the elemental beings within nature and talk to them. They saw the gods, the beings of spirit; they knew the reality of the Great God Pan. At the same time, individualised thinking broke into human consciousness as a new power and a new delight. That was the beginning of the growth of the faculty which led to a great scientific and technological age, but in order for that to develop, the faculties which could perceive the higher world had to die. This is represented by Odysseus putting out the single eye in the brow of the giant Polyphemus, for Odysseus is the great symbol for the development of individualised intellect in humankind. The opening sentence of *The Odyssey* states that 'Odysseus of many devices' has to go through all his adventures 'to find his own soul'. The story of Western humanity is symbolised in this great myth. To evolve our intellectual consciousness we have first to extinguish the faculty of supersensible vision. Then in freedom it may be reawakened.

The time is ripe for us to make the breakthrough back into the unity to which we truly belong and from which we descended. This is the moment in our long evolution for which the heavens have been waiting. But nothing may be done by the forces of light which would destroy or invalidate free will. So delicate is the technique evolved by the higher worlds to communicate with humankind that it is only in inner telepathic linkage that they can speak, and perforce that must be a quiet voice speaking to a stilled heart and mind. So long as we chatter in our minds and are fretful and anxious in our emotions, we simply cannot hear. Until we can learn to stop, listen and ultimately hear, a real link cannot be made by those above. This is the extraordinary paradox. All that they can do, apart from that, is to shock us. The disasters taking place in the world so frequently now may be a form of education—perhaps even staged by the higher beings. For we know well that death is the great teacher. Facing death, overcoming fear of it, passing through it ourselves, experiencing the loss of friends who are released by it and coping with death within the psyche many times during our life—all these are the great educative factors.

It looks as if we are reaching an age when immense change is afoot which may outwardly appear cataclysmic but which is a prelude to the great cleansing obviously necessary as a preparation for the inflooding of light. Certain messages from higher sources have indicated that the pressure of the forces of light may actually re-tilt the Earth, implying that through human negativity and the weight of materialistic thinking the planet has fallen away from its true axis. This would, of course, outwardly bring cataclysmic change, but those who have communicated this message say there need be no fear, since the cleansing operation will bring the possibility of a new golden age upon this planet.

Meanwhile, so disturbing is the world, so full of turmoil and danger, that it is of profound importance that we think ourselves into the realisation that you can't put new wine into old bottles. First the old bottles have to be smashed up and thrown away on the rubbish heap, in order that on a new vibratory level a more shining bottle may be produced to receive the outpouring of the waters of Aquarius, the wine of the spirit. We have to learn to think allegorically and apocalyptically if we are really to grasp what is happening. We may feel we are playing a part in the greatest experiment humankind has ever experienced. We are truly the hobbits of Tolkien's story engaged in the great battle between the forces of darkness and those of light, with the immensely important task of carrying that ring back to Mount Doom. For, if you remember, the moment the ring is returned to its source, the will power of the Lord of Darkness disintegrates. Sauron becomes impotent, and since it is his telepathic control of the goblin armies of darkness that gives them their enormous power, the moment his strength collapses that whole army is filled with confusion and terror and becomes paralysed.

That is what could happen. There can be true intervention on such a plane, and there could be a collapse of that which activates the powers manifesting so potently as confusion, cruelty and violence. Radio and television concentrate on that dark side of life and do not show the birth of a new spring that is taking place everywhere as the spiritual world view becomes understood and accepted.

I am tempted to interpolate a story here. Surprisingly enough, this is a military report from the *Guards' Gazette*, made by an intelligence officer in 1918 at the end of the First World War. The British lines were just holding with a limited number of men. The wall of defence was so desperately thin that they were endeavouring to simulate machine gun fire by rapid rifle fire. Against them the massed forces of the German army made the final attack. History has it that surprisingly the attack failed and the Germans retreated; the Allies rallied and counter-attacked, the German army broke and the war ended. The story reported as a result of the interrogation of a captured German officer and confirmed by several other prisoners was essentially as follows. Behind Bethune was an area of hills which had been plastered by German fire before the offensive began. Suddenly the fire was lifted and there was such silence that the men could hear a single lark singing. Then the Germans advanced, singing because they were so certain of triumph, for there was virtually nothing to stop them. The officer reported that his lieutenant pointed out to him some cavalry riding over the hills, all dressed in white and riding white horses—which seemed extraordinary because the British had not used cavalry for three years and they usually dressed in khaki anyway. The cavalry came forward into the range of fire of the German machine guns and shells at a steady walk trot, as on a parade ground, and not a man or a horse was touched by any of the fire. In front of them was riding a great figure of a man with an aureole of golden hair around his head, a great sword by his side, and his hands just gently controlling the reins. Then the German forces were seized with panic. The officer said: "There around me were men whimpering with fear, throwing away their rifles and arms and running. And I, an officer of the Prussian army, turned and fled, filled with fear. The German army is defeated, by the white cavalry. I cannot understand it; I cannot understand it. Defeated by the cavalry and their extraordinary leader."

That story was confirmed from various sources. At any rate, it suggests the possibility, in our matter-of-fact days, that strange events may still take place. To quote a quatrain from James Elroy Flecker:

*Awake, awake! the world is young*
*For all its weary years of thought.*
*The starkest fights must still be fought,*
*The most surprising songs be sung.*

It is easy for 'sensible people' to reject this talk about spiritual beings, but we begin to realise that anything could happen, that the world is full of mystery within mystery. It is all here, now. We are dealing with different vibratory levels which are all ever-present. The spiritual planes, outside time, are instantly wherever they choose to project themselves, and therefore this room can be thronged—and probably is thronged—with invisible beings whom we must consciously welcome. The exciting thing is that this concept of the different levels of vibration and frequency fits perfectly with advanced Einsteinian physics. This is the bridging point at which the thinking of the advanced physicists equates with that of the mystics. The great physicist Sir James Jeans said in the 1930s: "It begins to look as if the universe is an affair not of atoms, but of thought." And now the advanced physicists are talking in terms of higher levels of vibratory rate being realms of light, which are also realms of thought and being. They are formulating concepts about what they call the Thought-field and the Life-field—fields of consciousness organising the atomic structure within form and holding it in shape. These are fields into which human consciousness can also enter.

You remember how at school we played with the magnetic field. If we spread iron filings on paper and then turned on the magnetic field, they all leaped into beautiful vortices and patterns. Take that thought and imagine that we are the little iron filings. The difference is that the iron filing reacts automatically to the magnetic field, whereas the human unit can either react consciously to the organising field or wilfully refuse to react. See that each of these little entities, left to itself, full of its own egoism, spends its time colliding with the others, trying to get more for itself. The whole area, as we look down upon it, is in uttermost confusion, because individuals and groups are all grabbing what they can for themselves. We are caught up in passion and desire. Egoism is rampant; it is almost a field in itself. Now let us suppose that the scientist working above begins to turn on the magnetic field and it starts penetrating into the confused area, though in this experiment the force does not constrain but allows the tiny iron filings free choice. Those who choose to attune are at once filled with a new power and harmony.

The image is quite a good one, because it looks as if what the higher world is now doing is turning on the magnetic field. The light is flooding in and the power and the pressure rising. Therefore, within each of these particles there may be an inner conflict. They have the free choice as to whether they will refuse to let the field work in them and still continue their egoistic conflict, or whether they will let go and fall into alignment. What great power would arise if all those little human points dropped their egoism and came into alignment voluntarily! There would follow a rapid reordering of the structure of substance and society, and through it the channelling of power and creativity, which would lead to miraculous things that we cannot conceive of at the moment. This is what seems to be happening at present: we are working up to that moment when the magnetic field, so to speak, is fully turned on.

The process may be experienced as a mounting of tension. At present society is still shot through and through with egoism, desire and greed, and because we do not understand what is happening, the increasing pressure shows itself in confusion, in turbulent new movements, in anxiety, disturbance and violence and all the unpleasant manifestations of what people can do to each other. But realise that what may be happening is a building up of pressure to a point where something must break. We can't tell quite how, but that mounting tension, that dark tower, is surrounded and contained by forces of light which have an overview of the process and are watching and waiting for the moment when the dark centre collapses. Then it will be possible for the full force of the magnetic field to be turned on, and all who are attuned—or prepared to attune—will then fall into the new pattern. This could happen, as the apocalyptic passages in the Bible have said, 'in the twinkling of an eye'. It is from one moment to another that the field is fully turned on. There is much evidence that the higher worlds are now mounting the operation which is going to bring about the dissolution of the barriers between human beings. As we develop what the poet Coleridge called 'sacred sympathy', the egoism and ignorance which separate us will increasingly be overcome.

Realise that in the effort to bring about a united humankind, we do not need to rely simply on our own self-sufficiency. We must conceive this darkened, errant planet as surrounded by powers of Light who can bring it into line with the whole of the solar system and the galaxy. It is through human misconduct, misunderstanding and ignorance over the aeons that the planet and its working has gone out of line. It is said by many sources that this planet is a kind of channel through which much of the spiritual force of the universe must pass at some stage or another, but that through human action it has become a bottleneck. The blockage must be cleared away in order that the flow may continue. And again in the twinkling of an eye, when the blockage is removed, things could change—into we know not what. Hence the immense importance of what the Findhorn Foundation is trying to teach: a technique for living in the moment, a submission to divine guidance. As spiritual entities, we are beings possessed of will, thought and feeling, existing in time and therefore experiencing only this instant...and now the next...and now the next. The beings working with us are outside time on an eternal vibration. Therefore humanity is that point in the whole of nature where the timeless can impinge on and transform the world of matter—but only by energies poured in at this moment, the ever-fleeting *now*.

This new art is like a dance from second to second, moment to moment, into a future we do not and cannot know and yet with which we are called upon to cooperate creatively. It is an extraordinary paradox. All our preparation, learning of techniques, achieving of qualifications, may have little relevance to what the creative impulse really wants us to do. We imprison ourselves in our structures of belief, thought and learning, but are now called upon to learn quite a new form of creativity which moves from instant to instant, dedicated always to the inflooding of the light. When we are rightly attuned, these energies will bring an inner certainty as to what we must do, even if we have never done it before. That is why it has been stressed here in this spiritually oriented community that guidance must be found within each of us. To use Browning's words:

> *Truth is within ourselves; it takes no rise*
> *From outward things, whate'er you may believe.*
> *There is an inmost centre in us all*
> *Where truth abides in fullness; and around,*
> *Wall upon wall, the gross flesh hems it in,*
> *This perfect clear perception—which is Truth.*

We must learn to work with this inmost centre, so that we can be free to move lightly into an unknown future. The more things collapse outwardly, the more we may know that this is a preparation for the time when the old bottles are thrown away and the new wine is poured—and we are the channels.

To close, this great passage by the poet-playwright Christopher Fry summarises our present condition. It comes from the play *A Sleep of Prisoners*, in which six British prisoners of war are imprisoned in an empty church at night—a powerful symbol. They move through the night, quarrelling and bickering with each other and then one after the other is taken over and spoken through by some higher power. Meadows, the sergeant, speaks:

> *The human heart can go the lengths of God.*
> *Dark and cold we may be, but this*
> *Is no winter now. The frozen misery*
> *Of centuries breaks, cracks, begins to move:*
> *The thunder is the thunder of the floes,*
> *The thaw, the flood, the upstart Spring.*
> *Thank God our time is now, when wrong*
> *Comes up to face us everywhere,*
> *Never to leave us till we take*
> *The longest stride of soul men ever took.*
> *Affairs are now soul-size.*
> *The enterprise is exploration into God.*
> *Where are you making for? It takes*
> *So many thousand years to wake*
> *But will you wake, for pity's sake?*

# Chapter Six
# Earth Alive

*Onearth Conference, October 1979*
*'A Positive Vision for the 1980s'*

Let us stretch forth imaginatively, lift our consciousness and look down from the heights on to the Earth, that beautiful sphere shining blue and silver in the velvet sea of space, turning according to divine law through the depths of the heavens. Feel the wholeness of the life of the planet, in its pulsating, ever moving, ever developing vibration.

Think into the great forests. Feel the trees, a bridging point between Earth and the forces and energies of the heavens. Grasp the cycle of the water, running ever downward as it strives to enter the great liquid sphere of the oceans, but drawn upward in water vapour from lakes and streams, lifted into the clouds. Above the high cirrus clouds, water vapour actually dematerialises and moves over into the spiritual plane, to reform again in dew and snow, virgin matter coming back in exquisite form in the Earth realm of gravity.

Feel again into the forests and the balanced life of birds and animals and insects. Nature is in perpetual flow and movement of transformation, sometimes infinitely slow like the changing and moulding of the hills, sometimes almost visible as in the opening flower or the metamorphosis of the butterfly, sometimes actively observable in the forming and dissolving of the majestic clouds. The mind's eye can be cultivated to see beyond the limitation of the outward senses, to touch the very being within the form and unite with the idea underlying it till we are one in soul with the beings of nature. Through lifted inspiration, 'Earth alive' becomes a valid concept.

We are entering a momentous decade when change faces us on every level, in our society, our own consciousness and in the very structure of the Earth itself. Thus it is of profound importance to grasp the holistic world picture. That wonderful word 'holistic' includes both holiness and wholeness. The whole is holy. Healing is the restoring of harmony to the living whole. The emerging new age vision is imbued with the concept of the oneness of all life. The universe itself is seen as a vast continuum of consciousness, of creative thought of God. Humanity is in essence a spiritual being in a cosmos spiritual in its nature and origin. In both scientific and mystical knowledge, this conviction of oneness replaces the old materialism and brings a wider interpretation of evolution.

Central to this world view is the conviction that the Earth is essentially a living creature with its own breathing, sensitivity, bloodstream, glands and consciousness. Humanity is not a chance accident of natural selection but an integral part of the living organism of the planet. Once we grasp that the universe is Thought, then we see that the planet of matter and form is derivative from divine Idea. Archetypal creative Ideas, which are in essence Beings, are the dynamic source of all forms appearing in nature. This holistic view is not so much dogma, but rather an exploration into a realm of concepts and imagination, vast, immeasurable and infinitely thrilling.

There is a remarkable book by Kit Pedler called *The Quest for Gaia*, which greatly enhances an understanding of the idea that Earth is alive. He follows the research of James Lovelock in seeing the life processes of Earth as being driven by an Intelligence fully capable of recognising and repairing damage done to itself. It possesses an ancient wisdom, observes our actions and counters them when they go against its purposes. The living planet is a seething flow of movement and change, never still, yet always one, as with the pattern in a kaleidoscope. The Earth organism searches perpetually for balance and harmony, and its intelligence appears to be able to counter and stabilise any imbalance caused by human or cosmic factors. James Lovelock and Kit Pedler revive the Greek name Gaia, the Earth Goddess, as a true expression of the nature of this purposeful intelligence of the planet.

The sun's energy flow sustains life upon Earth. Some of the energy is stored, as when plants convert sunlight into life through photosynthesis—and the leaf may be seen as the perfect solar panel. There is always some leak in wasted heat, as in respiration and digestion; all energy used by living and non-living processes eventually degrades into irrecoverable waste heat. This waste, contends Kit, is the ultimate pollutant. All dynamic processes tend to disorder and entropy. Entropy is defined by *The Oxford English Dictionary* as "the measure of the degree of molecular disorder existing in a system, also determining

66

how much of the system's thermal energy is unavailable for conversion into mechanical work, expressed as a thermodynamic function." The natural systems of Gaia involve only low grade entropy or leak of waste heat, easily restored by the sun's power.

For aeons humanity lived in close harmony with nature and did little to disturb the earth processes. Even when we moved from a nomadic lifestyle to an agrarian culture, we caused little more entropy. But industrial civilisation and technology broke the close dependence on Gaia. As we began to rely on the stored solar energy of fossil fuels rather than direct solar energy, we created a massive quantity of entropic disorder. What we are suffering from now is not an energy crisis so much as an *entropy crisis*.

Spaceship Earth is an almost closed system which can recycle all its constituents and conserve energy. The processes of decay, breaking down 'dead' matter into humus, the matrix of new life, are indeed beautiful. But most of our actions are directly opposed to these cyclical processes of Gaia. In our quest for profit and progress through technology, we appear to have forgotten that our life and survival is entirely dependent on our working and living as part of Mother Earth. We are guilty of appalling entropy-waste. Over 70% of heat energy from electrical power stations goes to irrecoverable waste. Heat waste is the worst form of pollution and today, through massive entropy, we threaten the stability of the whole dynamic structure of nature.

But Gaia is not likely to fall under such treatment, for she has her own intelligence, quite ruthless, which knows how to take any blow, give to it and counter-attack with an irresistible strength which restores the imbalance. When the blows of technology become too serious, then the rebound by Gaia comes with accelerating speed.

The offensive capacity of the Earth is well illustrated through the way nature meets our drugs and pesticides. DDT, hailed as the wonder drug to remove malaria, actually calls forth the breeding of ever stronger forms of mosquito. Antibiotics result in what is called 'transferable drug-resistance', where bacteria somehow learn to use and *communicate* a survival mechanism, so that we merely kill off the weaker strains while nature brings about others ever stronger and more resistant. As Kit poignantly notes: "Nowhere has there ever been an attack in war which has as its final conclusion the creation of *more* enemy troops."

The Mind of Gaia is in a permanent state of evolution and revolution, continually transforming its own structure to maintain conditions

67

at an optimum for continuance of life processes. Through our technology we can now apparently free ourselves from the old rhythms of nature. But we can side-step and ignore the evolutionary processes of Gaia only for a short time. If we are to survive as a race, we must learn again to work with the great Being of Mother Earth. Gaia is counter-attacking; her anger is rising at our pollution of the planet. Sensitives tell us the etheric and elemental world of the nature spirits is turning against humanity in retribution. We, as stewards of the planet, have wholly lost the real sense of meaning of life on One Earth. Unless we can relearn to serve the whole of which we are integrally part, we are faced with disaster.

The emergence of the so-called alternative lifestyle is a trend full of hope. All over the country groupings are appearing which express the new vision of wholeness and the oneness of the living planet—Friends of the Earth, Men of the Trees and the Soil Association; conservation groups, biodynamic farming, organic husbandry and whole-food stores; meditation groups, health centres and healers; new books on the spiritual world view; new communities of which the Findhorn Foundation is perhaps the most significant, dedicated to the service of the whole for the glory of God; new schools and education consciously awakening the sense of cooperation, not competition—we could go on and on and the list is impressive. It is an astonishing manifestation of an impulse to creative oneness.

It is not necessary for all who give their service in these causes to acknowledge the spiritual nature of humanity and the universe. A quickening of the spirit is taking place everywhere. It works through the inner centre in us all and may use many who do not admit to the divinity within every form, but who nevertheless are truly servants of the divine awakening. The groups and cooperative ventures, presently somewhat dispersed and unorganised, are rapidly coming together into living association, heralding the birth of a new society, a Gaian society. They represent a drive to work with Gaia in creative harmony.

The concept of 'Earth alive' gives much greater meaning and purpose to what we are doing. In recognising Gaia as an entity and intelligence originating from the archetype of the Earth organism, Kit Pedler is doing much more than merely reviving an aspect of pagan pantheism. He is creating a myth for the post-industrial age.

If the race is to survive, says Kit, a post-industrial age is inevitable, for survival is impossible without continually adjusting our lives to the demands of the dynamic Earth organism. To quote from his book: "Industrial society completely opposes the aims and objectives of a planet-wide individual entity with purpose, intelligence and ability to change. Although it is impossible for us to oppose the natural currents and imperatives of this individual, it is possible for us to understand how these currents work and therefore to plan a way of life in accord with them. The industrial society with its lethal output of entropy is directly opposed to them. So it follows that the industrial society must be abandoned."

A Gaian lifestyle would involve abandoning many of the expensive entropic machines, relearning survival skills and radically changing our way of living. Thus *The Quest for Gaia* is subtitled *A Book of Changes* and goes into detail on ways of practical living to cut entropic waste from our lives. It is challenging to think about a post-industrial revolution. Kit suggests that computer technology is evolving what is almost a new species—the intelligent chip. A science fiction situation is conceivable in which computers could become so complex and powerful that they begin to treat humans as redundant or at best as their slaves. Super-technology may lead to a deskilling of the human being in a vast bureaucracy, which he calls the Cybernarchy.

Yet there is a more optimistic view. The silicon chip may bring about a revolution through breaking up the old drive of going to work to earn a living and may bring much greater leisure. Technology is bringing us ever nearer to the faculties of a spiritual being, able to communicate instantly with any part of the world, to see immediately what is taking place, to travel anywhere. For those with spiritual vision and working to form the new society, this can be a great advantage. The communication network unites humanity as one family. Right use of electronics with the vision of wholeness would greatly improve the human lot. But technical achievements of the human brain used with an undeveloped moral sense in a greedy materialistic setting will bring disaster. Is it possible that the spiritual worlds themselves are behind the invention of the silicon chip, in order to shake us out of our present rut and compel us to take creative responsibility for ourselves?

Modern micro-technology used without vision necessarily leads to catastrophe. If a transformation within human consciousness were to take place, then we might learn how to tame technology. Such inner transformation is therefore the major task for us all if we are to keep the situation in control.

Ultimately Gaia is undefeatable, since her intelligence can compel any part of her organism to come into harmony with her whole structure. And further—Gaia herself is part of the greater organism of the solar system, part of the living universe. The planets may be seen as comparable with the endocrine glands (macrocosm and microcosm). When one of these little organs goes sick, the whole body becomes diseased. Planet Earth has gone sick and dark through human avarice and ignorance and the unbridled ambition of humanity. How long do we expect the spiritual worlds to stand by and watch while the errant steward of Earth degrades life on the planet? It appears that Operation Redemption has been launched, an inflooding of energies of light, love and power which could, with human cooperation and channelling, bring about molecular change to depollute the planet.

This is the apocalyptic age when a transformation of humanity is envisaged and foreseen by the end of the century, at the threshold of the Aquarian Age. Those who will not accept this and insist on clinging to a society based on the old laws of greed and getting for self, could be swept away in the disasters which will inevitably take place when Gaia really awakens in her anger. Since catastrophe could be a manner of divine working, it could be used by the angelic worlds to cleanse the planet. Here is a power which nothing can withstand or defeat—no less than God in action.

It is said that the battle for the Light has already been won on the higher planes. The ultimate victory is certain, but how much suffering and disaster takes place on the Earth plane turns entirely on the degree of human intelligence and the necessary turn-about in human consciousness. Death, we know, is not the end, but a release into planes where souls will gravitate to those beings to whom they are attuned. Hence the supreme importance of grasping the Christ vision *now* while we are embodied. And since the power of the Cosmic Christ overlights and 'informs' all the material plane and the whole Earth, the knowledge will transform our entire attitude to 'Earth Alive'. We must learn to think wholeness, to realise the reality of the Earth Mother, to know that we are so much one with nature that our exploitation of the animal kingdom and the rest of nature is piling up for us an enormous karmic debt.

The new age movement is essentially Gaian in its holistic vision. This is how Kit expresses it: "Gaia is all of life and all of the rocks. Within the universal intelligence of the one single living Earth organism is the way to a genuine expansion of wisdom and an ultimate experience of beauty. Just as Gaia is conscious, so too are we conscious. If we truly want to know ourselves, then we must first know Gaia."

70

And again: "Know that the rational, logical, reductionist analysis of Nature is magnificently, splendidly and absolutely wrong; and know that the Cybernarch is alien, hostile and irrevocably other; those are the necessities for Gaian vision."

The emergence of the alternative lifestyle is the equivalent of the coming of spring, the innumerable new shoots bursting and burgeoning and discovering that together they constitute a new society, indeed a new Jerusalem, behind which is a Power and a Life which is ultimately and absolutely undefeatable.

# Chapter Seven
# Nature and Spirit

*3rd World Wilderness Congress, October 1983*

Let me begin with a poem by Gerard Manley Hopkins, written beside a
burn which runs into Loch Lomond in the great Scottish Highlands.
Let your imagination work with the images it calls up.

> *This darksome burn, horse-back brown,*
> *His rollrock highroad roaring down,*
> *In coop and in comb the fleece of his foam*
> *Flutes and low to the lake falls home.*
>
> *A windpuff bonnet of fawn-froth*
> *Turns and twindles over the broth*
> *Of a pool so pitch black, fell frowning,*
> *It rounds and rounds despair to drowning.*
>
> *Degged with dew, dappled with dew*
> *Are the groins of the braes that the brook treads through,*
> *Wiry heathpacks, flitches of fern,*
> *And the bead-bonny ash that sits over the burn.*
>
> *What would the world be once bereft*
> *Of wet and wildness? Let them be left,*
> *O let them be left, wildness and wet;*
> *Long live the weeds and the wilderness yet.*

Imagination is not mere fantasy and unreality. It is the first step into
initiation knowledge of the invisible and higher worlds. Remember
Keats' affirmation: "I am certain of nothing but the holiness of the
heart's affection and the truth of Imagination."

What is the real meaning of the burst of vision represented by the poets of the Romantic movement? I quote a fine statement by the mountaineer Martin Conway: "The revolution in our modern attitude towards natural beauty was accomplished by poets and painters....It was the romantic soul in man that first saw itself reflected in nature. The mountains have always been the same. It was a new eye that saw them."

Come with me now on a brief imaginative exercise. Go up into a high valley before dawn and look with the inner eye of imagination at the light behind the purple hills just before sunrise. Wait in that great silence. Now see the rim of the sun break the horizon and finally clear the mountain tops. The sun has risen.

But what nonsense is this? The sun doesn't *rise*. That is pre-Copernican thinking. The sun stands still and the Earth spins around it. Now go back to the same picture but with a new understanding. In your imagination roll the planet over into the sunlight. Speed it up till the sun is above us and on till the sun disappears and all the stars come out—a majestical roof fretted with golden fire. You are still grounded in your body, but in imagination your consciousness has embraced the whole globe. You can sense its weight and feel it turning and rolling.

Now, greatly daring, free yourself from your body to float out into orbit and look down upon the planet. See it as Edgar Mitchell did when he came out from behind the moon and saw the beautiful orb of blue and silver against the velvet background of space. At that moment he had a peak experience of knowing, noetically and with inner certainty, that the universe is mind, not mechanism. It is a living oneness. Your consciousness is expanding among the stars and the Earth is turning. Zoom out so that the Earth reduces to the size of a football. What has happened? Your consciousness has enlarged vastly. Realise in actual imaginative experience that your consciousness can be co-extensive with immensity. Furthermore, you can look round that Earth and see it three-dimensionally. Look at it in its beauty. Put out an etheric hand to touch it, let it turn within your extended hands and bless it. See that humanity is part of the planet, anchored into the world of gravity. Gravity is one pole, but everything has polarity. The opposite pole is one of expansion, lightness and levity. There is nothing except our own separatist thinking to stop us stepping out into the consciousness of the great Oneness. In a modest way, this is what we are now doing. Something immensely important happens when we exercise our true power of imagination. Wordsworth gave us a hint of this when he said,

73

"An auxiliar light came from my mind, which on the setting sun bestowed new splendour."

In the last three centuries, since Newton's time, we have developed the intellectual faculties of the left hemisphere of the brain, with its masculine organising power and its pride in controlling and even 'conquering' nature (a terrible phrase). But the price we have to pay is enormous. It is the atrophying and going dormant of the organs of perception associated with the right hemisphere of the brain, the feminine, sensitive, intuitive faculties which can apprehend the living oneness of life and spirit. Blake, that great visionary poet, tells us of this price when he talks of the "wrenching apart of the perceiving mind and what we perceive from their original indivisible unity, to produce an externalised, fixed, dead nature and a shrinking of our humanity from the boundless being of the Imagination, into the mortal worm of 60 winters and 70 inches long."

We have shrunk and withered like an uprooted plant, and have lost the 'being' within nature. But listen now to Wordsworth in the great poem *Tintern Abbey*, describing how, as a boy, nature to him was all in all.

> ...*the sounding cataract*
> *Haunted me like a passion: the tall rock,*
> *The mountain, and the deep and gloomy wood,*
> *Their colours and their forms, were then to me*
> *An appetite....That time is past,*
> *And all its aching joys are now no more,*
> ...*other gifts*
> *Have followed...and I have felt*
> *A presence that disturbs me with the joy*
> *Of elevated thoughts; a sense sublime*
> *Of something far more deeply interfused,*
> *Whose dwelling is the light of setting suns,*
> *And the round ocean and the living air,*
> *And the blue sky, and in the mind of man:*
> *A motion and a spirit, that impels*
> *All thinking things, all objects of all thought*
> *And rolls through all things....*

But you are still out in space. Now look at the Earth holographically. You know that when a holographic plate is shattered, every fragment contains the whole three-dimensional picture. When Professor Carl Pribram was lecturing once in America, he suddenly stammered and checked in the reading of his paper as the thought hit him—"My God, what if the whole universe is a hologram!" If indeed it is, it follows that every human mind is a tiny bit of the shattered plate. This reminds us of the myth of Osiris, the god who was cut up into a thousand pieces, to be set together by the goddess Isis. However, while the holographic plate is inert, we human beings, a little lower than the angels and crowned with glory and honour, have the unique task of carrying the divine gift of free will in order that we may become in time co-creators with God. We are that part of nature which can become consciously creative and therefore can, to some small degree, re-create the photograph in the cosmic hologram.

It must be a source of excitement for the angelic world to watch the planet Earth as human beings begin to be creative and overcome their destructive egoism and violence. For we are called on to realise, in time, the true archetype of the human being, that first concept formed in the divine mind before matter came into manifestation. We were the measure of all things, made in the image of God, with the ability to carry and focalise Thought, Will and Love; spiritual beings entering the temple of the physical body in order to experience and overcome the limitations of matter and the sense world. This of course involved, for the time being, the losing of the realms of spirit and the experience of separation and loneliness, cut off from the divine.

But we are now passing through the phase of separation. We are living in the time when humankind stands on the threshold, when our self consciousness can take a quantum leap into cosmic consciousness. In this training ground of Earth we are reaching a stage when, so to speak, we are preparing to enter the university. This is the intense excitement of our generation. We have recovered the concept of oneness. With our intellects, we have dissolved matter into energy. Our leading scientists now approach the next step, which is to realise that energy is alive, that it is an ocean of life, being and intelligence poured out from the divine source.

This is, of course, not new. We are recovering the vision of the mystics of all ages, the ageless, ancient wisdom both of the Orient and of our Western mystery traditions. The so-called Hermetic Wisdom, deriving from the Egyptian initiate, Hermes Trismagistus, laid down as first principle that the universe is mind, not mechanism, and that everything manifests the law of correspondences—as above, so below;

as in the macrocosm, so in the microcosm. The human being is the microcosm reflecting the macrocosm; in essence a droplet of divinity and therefore immortal and imperishable. The essential being, the I, always was and always will be and cannot possibly die, since it is an attribute of God. This immortal self is housed in the perishable body, truly a fantastic temple for the spiritual entity to operate in the heavy density of matter. This concept is of paramount importance in our death-ridden culture, and in this turn-about in consciousness we see that humanity is not an accident of chance natural selection, but is one of the great purposes of God.

We are now grasping the holistic world view, first put forward in the 1920s by Jan Smuts of South Africa. 'Holism' implies, by its spelling, that the whole is holy. We are recovering this concept, held virtually by every culture but our own and central to the secret knowledge of the mystery traditions. Therefore look again at our Earth in its beauty and conceive that it is truly a living creature, a being, an organism with its own breathing, bloodstream, glands, sensitivity and intelligence. We are an aspect of the intelligence of the planet. Furthermore, we must see that humanity is itself an organism, integrally part of the whole of nature. Ours is the first generation which could grasp this thought. Teilhard de Chardin's noosphere is a living body over the face of the Earth and we are each cells in the one great body. When cells in our physical bodies choose to ignore the programming of the whole and go off on their own, we call it cancer. Similarly, when human cells in the body of Earth act out of egoism, greed and violence, and go off on their own reckless way, the Earth itself becomes cancer-ridden. The disease is far advanced, though not necessarily terminal.

We are polluting the planet, physically, mentally and morally, to the extent that we could bring about the extinction of our civilisation in the years ahead. But a change is taking place. More and more human beings, cells in the body of humanity, are stopping in their tracks, appalled at what the rightful stewards of the planet are doing to their mother the Earth. They are pausing, awakening, attuning and re-orientating. This is what Teilhard called 'homing upon the Omega point', lifting ourselves above the murky atmosphere of emotion and egoism surrounding the Earth into the clear light of heaven, and realising our true nature. The great hope is that when a critical number of people have consciously taken this step, a new understanding could shoot through the world. For when individual human beings freely take this step in attunement, it is immediately possible for the powers of the angelic world to pour through them to cleanse and purify our polluted planet and to harmonise all life. Teilhard called it 'the wild hope that our earth is to be recast'. There was never such a time to be alive!

Now it is time to come back to Earth. Take a plunge into the atmosphere, and turn once more with the Earth, seeing the stars appear to swing around you. Now dive back into your waiting body. This is almost an alarming experience, for you are undergoing something like the drastic limitation involved in birth, descending from the widths of space into the sense world. And this could be a relief. As T.S. Eliot wrote: "Humankind cannot bear very much reality." The Earth, to you, is now flat and stands still, and the sun begins to rise and the moon to set.

What has all this to do with the preserving of wilderness in the living Earth? Because we are part of the Earth, we are not mere onlookers observing nature. We *are* nature and we represent an evolutionary point where nature becomes conscious of itself. As Wordsworth and the great poets of the Romantic Movement realised, nature is not fulfilled until human beings, the crown of creation, take the step in consciousness to grasp the Idea, the Being within the tree, the plant, the bird, the mountain. This gives new meaning to the statement in Romans 8: "The created universe waits with eager expectation for God's sons to be revealed," and to the opening of St. John's gospel: "In the beginning was the Word, and the Word was with God, and the Word was God...All things were made by him." First came the Divine Idea, the archetypal creative Thought, to be realised later in substance. The Divine Idea is present everywhere, expressed into nature's forms, but this world of being and spirit is invisible to the physical senses. It is through the eye of the mind that it is apprehended. The mind, as droplet of the eternal mind, can, to use Blake's words, "open the eternal worlds, open the immortal eyes of man inwards into the realms of thought, into eternity, ever-expanding in the bosom of God, the human imagination."

Now consider also the deeper significance of the magnificent achievements of the younger generation in the so-called adventure sports, in which great feats of enterprise, endurance and skill are accomplished in exploring the world. You do not need any particular mystique to enjoy mountaineering, skiing or gliding; your motive may be fun and sheer excitement. But if you start thinking holistically and realise that we are the point of consciousness of Earth, a deeper meaning is revealed in the great sports and their exploration of nature.

Through us, Earth herself is taking a step in her consciousness of the elemental world. In hang-gliding and free-fall, we relate closely to the element of air. In skin-diving, canoeing and surfing, we identify in consciousness with the element water. As we climb on rock and snow or explore great caverns, we relate to the element earth. The planet is waking up through us, for we are her point of advancing consciousness. When Wordsworth walked the Lake District in love of its beauty, he was awakening nature herself. Nature is not fulfilled until we take this step in consciousness. Her dormant spirit awakens as humanity recovers the Hermetic vision and begins to live by it.

This factor is not taken into account in our politics, economics or even ecology. There is of course no need for this mystique, but those people planting trees, stopping pollution and preserving the beauty of landscape and wilderness are all serving Gaia, the goddess of Earth. The so-called 'alternative lifestyle', which grows directly out of holistic thinking, is concerned with living in a way that serves the living Earth. It is conservation, with spiritual vision.

Holism implies, indeed, that there is a power of higher intelligence which could actually bring about molecular change to depollute the planet, but this will not happen without our invocation and cooperation, since we are instruments of freedom. Ours, however, is the initiative, and our age is one of real science fiction in which, through a time of change, almost anything is possible. Glory be!

To close I give you a poem which I dedicate to our distinguished guest at this Congress, Sir Laurens van der Post, that great and very human being. It is by a great mountaineer, Geoffrey Winthrop Young, who lost his leg in the First World War and then climbed the Matterhorn with an artificial leg. Such was the scale of the man. His poem is called *Envoy*.

*I have not lost the magic of long days:*
  *I live them still, dream them still,*
*Still am I master of the starry ways,*
  *And freeman of the hill.*
*Shattered my glass, e'er half the sands had run—*
*I hold the heights, I hold the heights I won.*

*Mine still the hope that hailed me from each height,*
  *Mine the unresting flame;*
*With dreams I charmed each doing to delight;*

I charm my rest the same.
Severed my skein, e'er half the strands were spun—
I keep the dreams, I keep the dreams I won.

What if I live no more those kingly days?
  Their night sleeps with me still.
I dream my feet upon the starry ways;
  My heart rests in the hill.
I may not grudge the little left undone;
I hold the heights, I keep the dreams I won.

# Chapter Eight
# The New Essenes

*A Workshop on 'The Essenes', 1981*

My interest in what might be called 'the New Essenes' was aroused by reading Edmond Bordeaux Szekely's remarkable little book *The Teachings of the Essenes: From Enoch to the Dead Sea Scrolls*. This makes the perfect commentary on the larger, more scriptural and poetical volume, *The Gospel of the Essenes*.

Szekely's presentation is exciting. It makes the whole vision come alive, allowing the Essene teachings to fire the heart with a new enthusiasm—a word which literally means 'possessed by a god'. It is clear that the Essene teachings are a very pure and developed expression of the Ageless Wisdom, the ancient Hermetic doctrine of holism which underlies and overlights all the approaches to esoteric knowledge in all the religions.

When we look at the historical Essenes we find a brotherhood deeply conscious of the spiritual nature of humanity and the universe. They were aware of the threats to social order through people's greed and egoism, and recognised that all human suffering was caused by deviation from divine law. They knew that the restoration of peace and harmony with the law in every aspect of living was essential.

Thus their lives were dedicated wholly to the service of God; human freedom was absolutely respected since they knew that the kernel of humanity was divine; and meditation, prayer and attunement were vital factors in everyday living. At dawn they communed with the Angels of the Earthly Mother, while at dusk they attuned to the cosmic energies of the Angels of the Heavenly Father. At noon they paused in their activities for the contemplation of the Sevenfold Peace. They recognised that the Earth was a living, sentient creature and the universe was a vast continuum of Mind. They knew that the oceans of

Thought, Life, Love and Will permeated all ethereal space and penetrated the world of matter. All is energy and, since these cosmic energies are alive, they were called the Angels. Our modern scientific knowledge is rapidly approaching this vision, so that no essential conflict remains between true science and mystical religion.

The Essenes spent their mornings in work, in organic agriculture, horticulture and forestry, and in creative craft for the community. This always had something of the character of a religious ritual since, in serving the plant world, the soil or the trees, one was working with divine beings, the devas and nature spirits. Thus it was the custom to work in silent communion and love in the gardens, forests and workshops. The work became a kind of active meditation always begun by attunement.

Today we can recover the sense of working with living bodies and energies in activities like the crafts. Contemplate what it really means to make furniture with wood, to spin, dye and weave wool, to raise a copper bowl or shape silver in jewellery. See the deep ritual of pottery—to take clay and 'throw' it into form, to cover it in mineral glaze, to put it into the sarcophagus of the kiln, to apply fire to bring on the moment of metamorphosis into shining colour and then to use it for communal meals, the breaking of bread made of God's good wheat. Every craft can be something of a religious experience as we work with the elements of earth, water, air and fire to shape form.

The lifestyle of the Essenes appears well balanced. Physical toil did not fill the whole day. After the morning's work, there was time for recreation, which may be seen as a development of the body temple. Once we admit to the imperishable, eternal nature of the spirit of humanity, the I AM within each of us, we see the body as a microcosm reflecting the macrocosm, truly a temple into which the divine spark can enter and in which it can operate in the heavy density of the earthplane.

Looking at today's world from the holistic world view, we can see that in athletics and the great sports the I AM of humanity is taking ever more intelligent control of our mobile temple, the divinely planned body. This vision adds to the significance of the Inner Game approach to tennis, skiing, golf and athletics. We see also that the so-called adventure sports represent the ever more conscious experiencing of the elements of earth, water and air. Those who practise the sports need not concern themselves with the spiritual world view, of course, but once this awakens within us we see a profound significance in this impulse of self-mastery. The great sports have something of an initiation mystery in their skills. The body is integrally part of all nature and the spiritual kernel within us is therefore doing something to activate and awaken the Being of Earth. The time of recreation in the day or week thus takes on ever greater meaning.

Part of the Essene working day was also given to study of literature and the great scriptures. This was no mere academic exercise. The Essenes saw that the great works of literature—of drama, poetry, fiction and scripture—were the achievements of advanced souls who could resonate with the beings on the higher planes and then crystallise their inspiration into the book or poem. Our task is to learn to read the great works of literature in such a way that we too can resonate with the living thought that underlies them. By entering the right way into the living ideas behind the printed word, we can unite with the eternal plane of the Creative Source.

A whole new manner of studying literature derives from this idea. Once admit that the realm of archetypal ideas, the ocean of the creative thought of God, is there and surging and shining on the eternal planes, and that mind in humanity is a pulse of the eternal Mind, then the use of literature should be as a gateway into expanding consciousness. This is much more than the normal academic study, which is inevitably an example of the 'onlooker consciousness'. We are dealing with the reality of living Ideas, which are truly thought beings who long to 'incarnate' within human thinking.

There is tremendous value in taking a great work of fiction and making the reading of it a kind of ritual by deciding to read, say, 15 pages at a certain time each day. For some weeks you then move in imagination through the life experience of other souls, lifted by literature out of your own mundane path of life. Right reading is essential to soul development. Never say, "I have no time for novels." Learn to use books as living teachers, through whom you can resonate with the thinking of the masters, for that which they have achieved in thought is present beyond time in ethereal space and is therefore ours for the finding in the eternal now.

The same kind of approach can be applied in all the arts, both in study of architecture, painting and music and in practise of the arts and crafts. This, as with the Essenes of old, must take its place in the true Work of the day. As the individual soul begins to explore the higher spiritual dimensions, it must endeavour to express its findings in art form. The spiritual world view gives the greatest of all themes for drama, ballet, poetry, mythology, painting, music. According to our capacity, each of us will find the need and power to convey the stupendous picture of the spiritual being of humanity, 'God begotten, God companioned, forever Godward striving'. The great myth of humanity needs perforce to be expressed in symbolic and art form, that we may understand our true nature and the purpose of our sojourn on Earth. And when humanity takes over its inheritance and re-unites with the realm of creative Ideas, we can foresee a new renaissance, a marvellous release of human potential.

Out of these concepts a new lifestyle is emerging. First we grasp mentally at the *idea*, seizing it out of the ether for its very beauty and learning to live with it in our thinking, looking at life in the light of it while yet reserving judgment. In this way we can explore the imponderable world where intellectual proof is usually impossible. Then the heart is fired with inner certainty and from that comes the action of the will and the limbs.

In our time a spiritual awakening is taking place, firstly in an expanding of thought to grasp the holistic concepts and then in the emergence of the lifestyle which reflects them. On a very wide front new centres and groupings are forming, cooperatives and communities, working together in service of Gaia the Earth Goddess and to the glory of God, the Father/Mother Being of the Heavens. The work being done covers a very wide spectrum—organic husbandry, food reform and nature cure, alternative technology, survival techniques, conservation in all its breadth, meditation, transpersonal psychology, crafts and the arts, new drama, adult education for the spirit, healing and all the complementary alternative therapies—and so on and on.

It is by no means necessary for all practitioners to grasp the great spiritual concepts of holism. The conservationists work to preserve Mother Earth, whether or not they recognise her as a living creature. But when we do take hold of the spiritual world view, the emergence of the alternative lifestyle takes on a new and thrilling significance. All over the country, as in the coming of spring, new and tender shoots are appearing, taking root and fed with the strength of the power of the spirit. We know that behind the coming of spring is a power that is absolutely undefeatable. So it is with the new age movement. A society is beginning to emerge based not so much on getting for self as on service of the whole to the glory of God, knowing that all the angelic energies are there to flower through us in co-creation.

The new Essene impulse is not dogma. It is a pure expression of their ancient wisdom re-emerging in our time in a form suitable for the age.

Two thousand years ago the Essenes offered a protective setting for the descent of the Christ. They cared for the holy family, and Jesus, John and John the Baptist went out as Essene teachers and initiates. Now in the age of the Second Coming we find the impulse re-emerging, doubtless through the reincarnating of many souls who were then associated with it.

The integrative vision of Szekely gives us the structure of thinking which we can use as a guide in what we are doing, not in any sense as a rigid doctrine. The working day of the Essenes gave a balanced discipline of practical work, creative craft and art, exercise of the body, a period of study of great masterworks, a time of teaching and learning and of recreation. And through it all is the sense of working closely with the nature spirits and the angelic worlds, with all activity dedicated to the glory of God, and with joy in the heart.

# Chapter Nine
# In the Beginning was the Word

*Onearth Conference, October 1978*

"In the beginning was the Word, and the Word was with God, and the Word was God. The same was in the beginning with God. All things were made by Him, and without Him was not anything made that was made. In Him was Life; and the life was the light of men. And the light shineth in darkness, and the darkness comprehendeth it not."

We meet shortly after the festival of Michael, and it is incumbent on us here to recognise that we are overlighted by the power of that great archangel known as the Lord of the Heavenly Forces upon Earth, the Wielder of the Sword of Light, the Countenance of the Christ and the Lord of Cosmic Intelligence. He it is who overlights the movement with which we are concerned. So I give you to begin with this thought by Adam Bittleston, showing how the power of the Word should enter our thinking, our feeling, our willing:

> *We need in the light of our day the eternal Light of God. When with our thoughts we seek this light, on the path which leads from the cave where thinking and seeing are shadows, into the fields of light, into the freedom of the heart, we shall meet Michael, who reveals how Christ awakens thinking that may serve God.*
>
> *We need in the light of our day the eternal Bread of God. When we seek within our hearts this bread, on the path which leads from the swamp, where feeling is dulled, into the heights of grace, into the realm of the Sun, we shall meet Michael, who reveals how Christ awakens feeling that may serve God.*
>
> *We need in the Soul of our day the eternal Wine of the Word of God. When we seek with our faith this wine, on the path which leads from the desert where the beasts are raging, into the world of angels, into the will of spirit, we shall meet Michael, who reveals how Christ awakens willing, that it may serve God.*

*We need in the strife of our day the eternal Peace of the Word of God. Seeking this peace with our whole being, on the path which leads from the nightmare of endless chaos into the order of heaven and the Father of all things, we shall meet Michael, who reveals how Christ awakens man that he may serve God.*

The Word is the creative power which can pour into form and is behind all forms. At the very outset we must grasp how all the splendour of the world, all the beauty of the universe, is the Word in action, the Word made flesh. Here that idea is expressed in a poem by Kathleen Raine entitled *Word Made Flesh*. Let your imagination work into the beauty and rhythm of all creation and the sense that everything works to divine law. There is one law which manifests in infinite diversity, down to the smallest and most delicate thing, and where anything deviates from this law, there is suffering. This is the great truth taught by the Essenes.

*Word whose breath is the world-circling atmosphere,*
*Word that utters the world that turns the wind,*
*Word that articulates the bird that speeds upon the air,*

*Word that blazes out the trumpet of the sun,*
*Whose silence is the violin-music of the stars,*
*Whose melody is the dawn, and harmony the night,*

*Word traced in water of lakes, and light on water,*
*Light on still water, moving water, waterfall,*
*And water colours of cloud, of dew, of spectral rain,*

*Word inscribed on stone, mountain range upon range of stone,*
*Word that is fire of the sun and fire within*
*Order of atoms, crystalline symmetry,*

*Grammar of five-fold rose and six-fold lily,*
*Spiral of leaves on a bough, helix of shells,*
*Rotation of twining plants on axes of darkness and light,*

*Instinctive wisdom of fish and lion and ram,*
*Rhythm of generation in flagellate and fern,*
*Flash of fin, beat of wing, heartbeat, beat of the dance,*

*Hieroglyph in whose exact precision is defined*
*Feather and insect-wing, refraction of multiple eyes,*
*Eyes of the creatures, oh myriad-fold vision of the world,*

*Statement of mystery, how shall we name*
*A spirit clothed in world, a world made man?*

The human being as archetypal Idea is first in creation, though last
to appear in the ladder of physical evolution. For God said, "Let us
make man after our own image"—male-female created he them. How
naive it is to think that this body is the human being and that God is an
old man with a long beard somewhere behind the stars. God is ubiquitous—an invisible, universal, spiritual power, a great being of thought,
will, love and creativity. If he is to make a microcosm, a small version,
of himself, will it not also be a spiritual being: deathless, universal, a
strand of the great ocean of life? That is the human being—God begotten, God companioned, forever Godward striving, needing to take on a
physical form as the basis for the action of thought, feeling, will and
creativity while operating in the field of gravity on the training ground
of Earth.

Although we have been given free will, most of us have never done a
really free deed, for when we are tied to habit, to feeling, to emotion, we
are not free. Most of the things we invent or think we discover have
already been imagined in nature. Very few of our inventions are not
already thought of by the Word. We simply rediscover them. For instance, wasps had made paper for millions of years before we 'invented'
it. Most of our inventions and architecture are merely an externalisation of the archetypal body, for the body is truly the temple into which
the spirit can descend. Thus, our creations are often an image of that
which is already planted within the microcosm of our own body. In this
light it is most interesting to consider the inventions which launched
the industrial revolution. First came the steam engine, which can be
seen as an externalisation of the digestive or metabolic system, using
heat to convert matter into power so as to drive the machine. Next we
invented the internal combustion engine with its much subtler interplay of air and liquid, which strangely compares with the rhythmic
system of heart and lungs. Now comes the phase of electronic inventions, reflecting the central nervous system. The computer and the
robot become an astonishing parody of the human being and our communications network begins to turn into something of a global brain.

What we have not done—and I hope never can do—is actually to invent life.

In all this, see that the fantastic design of the human body contains the wisdom of the universe and that in our inventions we are simply externalising this wisdom. Indeed, it is the tragedy of modern humankind that, having taken what is in ourselves and reflected it in our inventions, we stand lost and soulless in the middle of a vast and complex collection of machines. What we are now striving to do is recover the true human being.

It is a profound spiritual truth that at the time of the Renaissance we were entering the period of glory and tragedy when we would discover and explore the sense world but lose ourselves as spiritual beings. We took the dive and the divine world, watching, took the risk that we might become so embedded in materialism and the outward senses that the very organs of perception of God and the Higher World would atrophy and become dormant, making the spiritual worlds no longer visible to human vision. And that indeed is what happened in the three centuries following Newton.

The concept of levity as the polar opposite of the force of gravity dropped out of human consciousness as the modern mind developed. Dr Ernst Lehrs, author of the important book *Man or Matter*, discovered a thesis published by the Academy of Florence called 'Contra Levitatem', which expressly stated that no longer was it valid for a science based on observation to speak of levity as the opposite of gravity and of equal rank with it. An explanation of the universe has been built up based solely on the concept of gravity, forgetting this greater truth that first in the vision of creation came levity—life, lightness and warmth. The manifestation of form is the interaction of the two forces of gravity and levity at their meeting point on the surface of the Earth. Take that thought and look at nature in the light of it.

There comes to mind a delightful remark made by John Ruskin, that great 'reader' of nature: "Newton told us, or was supposed to have told us, how the apple fell, but he has done nothing to explain to us what put the apple up there." And William Blake wrote:

*Now I with a four-fold vision see*
*And a four-fold vision is given to me,*
*Four-fold in my extreme delight,*
*And three-fold in soft Beulah's night,*
*And two-fold always. May God us keep*
*From single vision and Newton's sleep.*

He dared to call the Newtonian world view a form of sleep because it was a narrowing of vision. Thus, as Eddington put it, we have chosen to investigate nature with only one sense, the sense of sight, and that as if we were one-eyed, colour-blind pointer readers. The triumphs of the modern intellect and the glories of our technology are achieved at the price of losing our vision of the spiritual worlds and the workings of divinity in nature.

"May God us keep from single vision!" We have become mere spectators, onlookers observing and controlling nature. We don't belong any more. Wordsworth expressed the desperate sense of loss in his famous sonnet:

> The world is too much with us. Late and soon,
> Getting and spending we lay waste our powers.
> Little we see of Nature that is ours.
> We have given our hearts away—a sordid boon.
> This sea that bares her bosom to the moon,
> The winds that will be howling at all hours,
> And are upgathered now like sleeping flowers,
> For this, for everything we are out of tune,
> It moves us not. Great God, I'd rather be
> A pagan suckled in a creed outworn
> So might I, standing on this pleasant lea,
> Have glimpses that might make me less forlorn,
> Have sight of Proteus rising from the sea,
> Or hear old Triton blow his wreathed horn.

We are now, however, poised at the threshold of the counter-movement, when human consciousness, having gone through this depth of matter, is awakening once more to the vision that in the beginning was the Word, and that all things were made by God, and 'without him was not anything made that was made'. We are breaking through into a realisation of the oneness of the Earth within the living organism of the solar system. We are becoming aware that we have been violating the Law. Humankind is a hierarchy of spiritual beings, eternal and imperishable, set in the field of gravity. We are the meeting point between two worlds, the point of consciousness at which evolution has become reflective. Through the development of the left hemisphere of the brain—the masculine intellect—we have been led into deviation from divine law, which has resulted in all the disaster and suffering now coming upon us. We have to learn to stop violating the law and consciously come into line once more with the workings of God. We are given the opportunity of becoming free beings and acting in free creativity. What a delight it will be to the Creator to be able to see a point in his creation which itself becomes creative!

Anything can happen once we wake up, for we are realising the unlimited potential of the human being. When astronaut Edgar Mitchell came out from behind the moon and saw the beautiful planet Earth—his home—he had the peak experience of knowing with absolute inner certainty that the universe was Mind, shot through and through with the creative thought of God. He thereupon dedicated his life to the service of this truth. Then he was hit by a thought: "My God, on that lovely planet people are murdering, torturing and deceiving each other and planning and fighting wars. They are spilling blood in cruelty and violence, caught in a morass of sensuality." But then he saw the potential of humankind, which we have hardly begun to touch emotionally and intellectually. In the composite volume written by him and his colleague Jean Houston there is this passage:

> *If we are to continue as a species we need a revolution in being and an evolution in cultural paradigm achieved by becoming what we have the demonstrable capacity to be. We may be able to mobilise these energies in an entirely new way, in terms of what might be called a 'psyche-naut' programme—not a mere astronaut programme—the aim of which is to follow the initiatives of the myths and to put the first man on Earth. Now the walls have tumbled down and what is revealed is a vastness, a perspective of human possibility, a hopefulness which could not be seen when our vision was contained. Man unfolding, man emerging, man gaining access to the great latent powers of his body, mind, psyche. This must be the new image of man if we are to survive our time. Man already has the potential to become fully human. This is the promise of the myth arising in our time, the image that can energise man to accomplish his transformation and so become a deserving trustee of his own evolution on Earth.*

This is the great task we are all engaged in. Our new age movement is not somebody's nice social plan to produce a more pleasant society, but the channelling of and creative working with the oceans of divine energy made by God in his primal move into creation. Here we must stretch our minds into the concept of the Almighty dividing and sub-dividing himself into oceans of creative being and heavenly energy—the oceans of thought, wisdom, will, love and personality and the great hierarchies from the Cherubim, the Seraphim and the Thrones through the Principalities, Mights and Powers down to the Archai, or time spirits, the Archangels and Angels. And humans are made a little lower than the angels, because we are given the potentiality of free will. So we are called upon to become creative, not for the aggrandisement of our own ego or for our own gain but for humanity as a whole and for God.

In our imagination we have to grasp the inpouring of living Ideas into form, which in due time is broken down again, dying in order that spirit may be re-released into the timeless world to which it belongs. Therefore chaos is necessary. Every form must have its time of returning to formlessness, as in every seed—which is matter returned to 'chaos' and therefore ready to receive the inpouring of the creative Idea. This holds good throughout nature and in society. We are watching and experiencing a society turning to chaos. That is the essence of change, that outward forms dissolve so that the inner Idea, the spiritual power, shall be released to re-form. This is the adventure of soul metamorphosis. As we awaken to the truth that we are eternal spiritual beings who can dedicate ourselves to the service of the whole as conscious instruments through which the higher worlds can channel themselves, so we expand in consciousness and move into levels upon levels of light. This is not an ascetic picture of a cold and arid puritanism, but an invitation to a new form of exploration so full of joy and wonder that it is beyond our ordinary imagination to conceive it. We may realise that this is the challenge and destiny of our time. It is touch and go whether life is to survive upon this planet, or whether catastrophe is to come upon us through our ignorance, fear and folly. We know there is no death for the eternal being within us and therefore, if we are wiped out by bomb or flood, we shall rally upon another vibratory level round those great beings to whom we are attuned. Thus if we are attuned to the forces of Michael and the Christ, it is under those banners that we shall rally to form a new civilisation on another level. If we are attuned to the older laws of violence, revenge, hatred and fear, we shall be led to some other planetary level to be shepherded by the Christ power and given the chance for redemption on a later round. So ultimately all is well.

Michael, Lord of the Cosmic Intelligence, is a reality, but there is also Ahriman, the Lord of Darkness, the satanic force denying the spirit, who is working to master the human, over-masculine intellect, and Lucifer, the fallen angel who works to inflate our egoism and desire for power. Those of us feeling a new spiritual awakening are trying to attune to the power of Michael, which is the thinking of the heart and bearer of the Christ impulse. Our true humanity which can apprehend the living Oneness lies in the male/female balance of the two hemispheres of the brain. Therefore our movement is concerned with the flowering of the spirit through the Michaelic impulse entering the heart. We recognise Michael as the great archangel who is overlighting our civilisation and this epoch of the Second Coming of the Christ—whatever form that majestic event may take. This is what we are called upon to understand.

I shall close with the splendid invocation to the archangels which, though given by Eusebius in about 200 AD, is very fitting for our own time:

*Ye hosts angelic, by the high Archangels led,*
*Heavenly powers beneficent, mighty in the music of the Word,*
*Great ones entrusted with the sovereignty of infinite celestial*
                                        *spheres,*
*Marshalling the cherubim and the flaming seraphim;*
*Ye, O Michael, Prince of Heaven,*
*And Gabriel by whom the word is given,*
*Uriel, great archangel of the Earth,*
*And Raphael of healing ministry*
*To those who yet in bondage are,*
*Guide our footsteps as we journey*
*Onward into Light Eternal.*

# Chapter Ten
# Towards a New Renaissance

*Spring Festival of the Arts, Easter 1983*

It is very appropriate that on this Easter Sunday we open a Festival of the Arts and begin it with a talk on the New Renaissance. We are cosmic beings at one with the entire universe. But being born on Earth into the imprisonment of the five senses is a drastic limitation—a kind of death, in fact. Blake summarises the human situation in these words: "There has been a wrenching apart of the perceiving mind and what we perceive, from their original indivisible unity, to produce an externalised, dead nature and a shrinking of our humanity from the boundless being of our Imagination into the mortal worm of 60 winters and 70 inches long."

In this context we begin to see what resurrection really means. The resurrection is not just a historical event that took place two thousand years ago. It is a step we are each individually called upon to take. The real teaching of Christ is that he *is* the Oneness, the kingdom, and that we are heirs to that kingdom.

See what he says of himself in the *Gospel of St Thomas*. "I am the All, and the All came forth from Me, and the All exists in Me." "You have lost the living one and speak about the dead." "When you make the two one, I am there"—an interesting variant on "When two or three are gathered in My name, there am I in the midst of them." "When you make the two one"— when you overcome the separation —"I am there." "I am the kingdom, and the kingdom is in me, and the kingdom is in you." "I am the resurrection and the life" (not "I am resurrected and alive").

This apocryphal Gospel of Thomas is an extraordinary document. It consists of 120 aphorisms of holism and is quite simply the Oneness doctrine. We usually write off doubting Thomas as one who wouldn't believe his Lord had risen, but the truth is that he was the *only* one who had grasped who his Lord was. He *knew* that Christ *was* the Oneness. Thomas did not doubt that his master had resurrected; rather he was the only one who knew absolutely that his master couldn't possibly die because he was Life—and he was bewildered.

There is a lovely description of when Thomas sees the Lord and calls him 'Master', and Jesus says, "I am not thy master, for thou hast drunk, nay, thou hast become drunk from the bubbling spring which I have released." He then leads Thomas aside and says three words to him, and when Thomas returns to the other disciples, they ask, "What did the Lord say to you?" And he answers, "If I told you what he said, you would pick up these stones and throw them at me and the stones would turn to fire and burn you up." He never tells us what the three words were! But it seems clear they were the equivalent of the oriental concept of "That art Thou". They must have been "I am you" or "We are one", because he saw what Christ was. It is not surprising that Thomas later went to India, because there he found a civilisation which could grasp the wholeness picture.

It is this wholeness picture to which we are now returning and the great step we are called upon to take is to move beyond sense-bound thinking and expand our consciousness into the whole. This step, if we can take it, will overcome the vast fallacy of materialism which has made the universe dead for us, and will enable us to enter the world of life.

The materialistic doctrine we have lived with for the last three centuries has lost the vision of the living universe. We have narrowed, we have shrunk, we have destroyed the living universe by our thinking. As D.H. Lawrence says, "The universe is dead to us, and how is it to come alive again? ...How...are we to get back to the grand orbs of the soul's heavens that fill us with unspeakable joy?" And he says there are two ways of knowing for humanity: knowing in terms of apartness —which is mental, rational and scientific; and knowing in terms of togetherness—which is religious, poetic and artistic.

We have to add a third way, which is the true marrying of both approaches, for both have their part. What we need to be concerned with in today's world is the redemption of thinking, the lifting of thinking out of separation by intensifying it into what Blake calls Imagination, lifting it beyond sense-bound, brain-bound thinking and back into the universe.

We have to realise that the human being is not just 'a mortal worm'. We are each a droplet of divinity, sojourning in the temple of the body, which is a microcosmic reflection of the Thought of God. The five senses enable us to operate on this plane effectively—but when we look through them alone, the world goes dead. We lose the spirit in nature; we lose the elemental world and the kingdom of the great god Pan; we lose the angels and archangels; we even lose and doubt God. The function of the Imagination is to allow us to recover our relation to the invisible kingdoms and to grasp the real truth behind form. This is the real resurrection, the real rebirth: lifting and expanding our consciousness into the greater world to which we truly belong, and discovering Christ as the centre of it all.

What, then, about the Renaissance, that extraordinary phenomenon in the 15th century which resulted in an immense burst of creative energy? If we look at history as the story of the evolution of consciousness, we see that it is a story of the immortal, eternal Ego of humanity constantly dipping into matter to learn the lessons that Earth offers. Earth is our great training ground as we develop toward freedom, and through the aeons we have descended deeper and deeper into the physical senses.

In the 15th century in Europe, the Ego of those of us in the West took the final step into the senses and the physical body. In a new way we began to look out from our eyes, to listen through our ears, to observe the beauty of our body and to explore the world, and it released an immense amount of creative energy and egoism. The simpler history books see the Renaissance as being brought about by such inventions as the mariner's compass or Galileo's telescopes. In fact, the reverse is true. The Renaissance was the result of a profound change in consciousness, both psychological and spiritual, in which the Ego identified with the body. What it meant was that we lost ourselves as spiritual beings; we plunged ourselves into the imprisonment of the senses. This may be seen as a tragic loss, and the seers and adepts of the time must have known it. I even have some sympathy with the old bigots who wouldn't look through Galileo's telescopes in case they had to admit that Copernicus was right when he said that the Earth was not the centre of the universe with the sun revolving round it. He could prove that the Earth moved around the sun.

But there is something delightfully simplistic about the Copernican world view. It does not have the whole truth. To use an analogy, it is as if we were to go into a theatre and be shown how the lighting and curtains and acoustics work, and how the stage is built and how the sounds are electronically controlled. "But I want to hear *Hamlet*," we say, and are told that doesn't matter; what matters is how it all works. In other words, we have forgotten the play. We have lost humanity. But the real truth is that humanity *is* the centre of the universe. One of God's purposes is to have part of creation itself become creative, in freedom. The real drama being enacted is inspired not by the Copernican picture, but rather by the vision that humanity is truly the purpose and centre of it all. We are the great experiment of the gods, and our artistic expression is our realisation and experience of the wonder of our own organism, and our potential for free creation in the world of form.

It is interesting that the artistic expression of the Renaissance is almost wholly spiritual. It is as if the higher worlds were making a tremendous affirmation of our spiritual nature and saying, "Look, you people, you are diving into the tomb of materialistic thinking. You are going to spend some centuries lost to the spiritual world as you explore your materialist discoveries, so before the curtain closes we will give you the true picture of humanity." The great art of the Renaissance gives us this perspective.

What is happening now is that we have come to the same threshold that we reached in the 15th century, but from the other direction. We are going through what Blake called the movement from Innocence to Experience and on to Imagination. From Eden we took the plunge into the world of the senses, losing the spiritual world but thereby gaining freedom, and the choice before us now is whether we go down to a new bestiality or reverse the process and come back, not to the Garden of Eden, for we can never reclaim the same innocence, but on to the New Jerusalem.

We are on the threshold of re-entering the world of the Creative Ideas, of stepping into the wholeness picture, remembering that we are immortal spirit and claiming the kingdom to which we are rightful heirs. It is a tremendous step, one which will transform society and on which the very salvation of humanity may depend.

How can we get the message across? Intellect is beginning to grasp it. The most advanced scientists are now talking essentially the same language as the mystics and adepts of the mystery wisdom. But it is primarily through the arts that it is communicated. Through the arts we externalise our inner experience of the wonderful human organism. Above the temple of Delphi the Greeks carved the statement, "Man, know thyself, and thou shalt know the universe." This means nothing to the materialistic consciousness, but to the consciousness that is one with the whole it is perfectly understandable. Through the holistic vision we learn that the body in its form and evolution contains all the secrets of the universe; also that the real human being, a little lower than the angels, is as wide as the starry heavens, for he/she is contained in the zodiac and the crystal spheres of the planets. So the counter-affirmation holds good as well: "Man, if thou wouldst find thyself, seek in the universe."

Architecture may be seen as the externalisation of our experience of the skeleton and its harmonics. Just as our bodies are the temple of our spirit and allow us to inhabit a material planet, so a temple is a structure which enables a god to operate in the heavy density of matter. Sculpture is the expression of our experience of the etheric body, the body of vital forces. We have reason to think that when the Greeks did their great carvings of the human figure they were not in fact using models; rather, with their inner eye they were able to experience the etheric body, the idealised form or archetype of the human body, and to reveal it and give it shape. Then in dance, the wonderful mobile temple of the body is able to express truths through movement, in a kind of living sculpture.

The next stage is the astral or emotional body, the soul body, which expresses itself in colour, through painting. And finally our spiritual being expresses itself in music and poetry, so that in the whole range of the arts we have the externalised picture of humanity.

To approach the arts in this way is to allow them to awaken our spiritual awareness and help us make the next step in consciousness. It lifts us right beyond the mere study of art history to see the spiritual significance of what is being expressed. Art history alone, though essential to us, may stop short at an intellectual interpretation and fail to open spiritual knowledge.

What a theme for the arts today! In the holistic world view we have a picture and a story of the most profound significance for modern humanity. We have to convey the concept of a spiritual being incarnating into the body temple in order to take the great evolutionary step in consciousness and freedom, to become a co-creator, a veritable child of God. In Blake's phrase, "We are set on Earth a little space, that we may learn to bear the beams of love."

And this concerns our generation, for these last decades of the 20th century contain the potential for transformation, personal and planetary. Intellect alone may fail to comprehend it. The arts can appeal directly to the 'thinking of the heart', the true Imagination. The occult (hidden) truths can be told in painting, drama, sculpture, ballet, dance and eurythmy, poetry, music and architecture.

We may be on the threshold of a new Renaissance. Remember that the creative energy of the 15th century Renaissance was released through the evolutionary step which *lost* to humanity its spiritual nature. It enabled us to discover and explore the physical world (and this indeed was the destiny of the West). Now we stand on the threshold when a great step can be taken by the individual from mere self-consciousness to cosmic consciousness. We are re-entering the plane of the Creative Ideas. Once we do so, we unite with a living force which must express itself in human thinking and above all in the arts as a new mythology emerges.

It has been well said that "Genius is the most effective channel for the creative source." We may prophesy the advent of a renaissance in the arts which could well outshine the glories of the earlier Renaissance, since its driving force will be in creative cooperation with the Divine Ideas. What a possibility! It is no less than a second birth, a resurrection, an inflooding of the light of the Cosmic Christ who overlights all humanity and *is* the living Oneness.

# Chapter Eleven
# The Poetry of the Living Earth

*'Earth Sings': A Festival of the Arts, October 1981*

The poets have always known the wonderful truth. Listen to Wordsworth, that great visionary of nature:

> *By one pervading spirit*
> *Of tones and numbers all things are controlled,*
> *As sages taught, where faith was found to merit*
> *Initiation in that mystery old.*
> *The heavens, whose aspect makes our minds as still*
> *As they themselves appear to be*
> *Innumerable voices fill*
> *With everlasting harmony.*
>
> (from *The Power of Sound*)

And Dryden:

> *From harmony, from heavenly harmony*
> *This universal frame began;*
> *From harmony to harmony*
> *Through all the compass of the notes it ran*
> *The diapason closing full in Man.*
>
> (from *A Song for St Cecilia's Day*)

And the passage from *The Merchant of Venice* when Lorenzo speaks to Jessica under the stars in Belmont:

> *Look how the floor of heaven*
> *Is thick inlaid with patines of bright gold.*

*There's not the smallest orb that thou beholdest*
*But in his motion like an angel sings,*
*Still quiring to the young-eyed cherubins;*
*Such harmony is in immortal souls,*
*But while this muddy vesture of decay*
*Doth grossly close us in, we cannot hear it.*

Now listen to some lines by Anna Kingsford about the nature of the poet:

*The poet hath no self apart from his larger Self. His personality is Divine; and being Divine it hath no limits.*

*He is supreme and ubiquitous in consciousness; his heart beats in every element.*

*The pulses of the Infinite Deep of Heaven vibrate in his own; and responding to their strength and their plenitude, he feels more intensely than other men.*

*Not merely he sees and examines these Rocks and Trees; these variable waters and these glittering peaks.*

*Not merely he hears this plaintive wind, these rolling peals.*

*But he is all these, and when he sings, it is not he—the Man—whose voice is heard; it is the voice of all Manifold Nature herself.*

*In his voice the Sunshine laughs; the Mountains give forth their sonorous Echoes; the swift lightnings flash.*

*The great continual Cadence of Universal Life moves and becomes articulate in human language.*

Let me now give you a poem from a distinguished modern poet, Kathleen Raine. Here she is seeing into the realm of the creative archetypes, the living Ideas from which all visible form derives. First the Divine Mind pours out the Ocean of Thought. Then out of these Ideas the plane of material form is crystallised. Behind every form there exists this ocean of living being:

*Pure was I before the world began,*
*I was the violence of wind and wave,*
*I was the bird before the bird ever sang.*

*I was never still.*
*I turned upon the axis of my joy,*

*I was the lonely dancer on the hill.*

*The rain upon the mountainside,*
*The rising mist,*
*I was the sea's unrest.*

*I wove the web of colour*
*Before the rainbow,*
*The intricacy of the flower*
*Before the leaf grew.*

*I was the buried one,*
*The fossil forest,*
*I knew the roots of things;*
*Before death's kingdom*
*I passed through the grave.*

*Times out of mind my journey*
*Circles the universe*
*And I remain*
*Before the first day.*

The whole mystery is contained in that poem, as also in the opening verses of St John's Gospel: "In the beginning was the Word and the Word was with God and the Word was God. By Him all things were made." We grasp the conception of the vast Oneness of life. The universe is one living whole, Earth is an integral being, and humanity —the crown of nature—is that point where nature becomes self-conscious. In the last three centuries we have so developed the masculine faculty of rational, intellectual analysis that the more intuitive feminine faculties which can apprehend the living Oneness have gone dormant and have atrophied. So the spiritual worlds have simply disappeared for us. We have become mere observers.

Our task now is to overcome this onlooker consciousness and once more experience the sublime truth that all nature is one and that the universe is Mind. So Francis Thompson writes in his somewhat diffuse poem *Mistress of Vision*. I quote only a few lines:

*Where is the land of Luthany?*
*Where is the tract of Elinore?*

> *I am bound therefor....*
> *When to the new eyes of thee*
>    *All things, by immortal power*
>    *Near or far*
>    *Hiddenly*
>    *To each other linkéd are,*
> *That thou canst not stir a flower*
> *Without troubling of a star;*
> *....Seek no more!*
> *Pass the gates of Luthany, tread the region Elinore.*

Elinore is an emotive name for the magical realm of the spirit. There is of course an obvious danger that reciting such poems with feeling can masquerade as spiritual knowledge! Yet the poetical vision does give a clue to our making the breakthrough to universal consciousness. For most people the world is a mass of separate things, looked at by our separated self. There is the oak tree, there is the flower, there the star, and here am I. We have lost the sense of oneness. Here is a remarkable outburst by D.H. Lawrence:

> *The universe is dead for us, and how is it to come to life again? 'Knowledge' has killed the sun, making it a ball of gas, with spots; 'knowledge' has killed the moon; it is a dead little earth fretted with extinct craters, as with smallpox; the machine has killed the earth for us, making it a surface, more or less bumpy, that you travel over. How, out of all this, are we to get back to the grand orbs of the soul's heavens, that fill us with unspeakable joy? How are we to get back Apollo and Attis, Demeter, Persephone and the halls of Dis? How even to see the star Hesperus or Betelgeuse? We've got to get them back, for they are the world our soul, our greater consciousness, lives in. The world of reason and science, the moon, a dead lump of earth, the sun, so much gas, with spots: this the dry and sterile little world the abstracted mind inhabits. The world of our little consciousness, which we know in our pettifogging apartness, in the mean separateness of everything.*
> *When we know the world in togetherness with ourselves, we know the earth hyacinthine or plutonic, we know the moon gives us our body as delight upon us, or steals it away. We know the purring of the great gold lion of the sun, who licks us like a lioness her cubs, making us bold, or else, like the red angry lion, dashes at us with*

102

*open claws. There are many ways of knowing, there are many sorts of knowledge. But the two ways of knowing, for man, are knowing in terms of apartness, which is mental, rational, scientific, and knowing in terms of togetherness, which is religious and poetic.*

That was written in the 1930s. Now we are realising that there is a third way to knowledge which is the uniting of scientific thinking with mystical vision. By intensifying our thinking and our imaginative vision, we can open ourselves to the world of living Idea and Being within the apparently separated forms. The most advanced scientific minds in our day are arriving at the same understanding of the great Oneness. Indeed Shelley wrote: "Poetry is the impassioned expression on the face of science." At one of our annual Wrekin Trust conferences on 'Mystics and Scientists', professor Charles Tart of the University of California declared: "There is no conflict between science and religion. The conflict is between dogmatic people, between second rate scientists and second rate mystics. There is only conflict between arrogance and humility, between closed mindedness and open mindedness."

Now we must bring in the father of modern poetry, Gerard Manley Hopkins. Here is a wonderful sonnet called *Hurrahing in Harvest*. Hopkins was acutely conscious of the Living Christ present in the whole of nature:

*Summer ends now; now, barbarous in beauty, the stooks arise*
  *Around; up above, what wind-walks! What lovely behaviour*
  *Of silk sack clouds! has wilder, wilful-wavier*
*Meal-drift moulded ever and melted across skies?*
*I walk, I lift up, I lift heart, eyes*
  *Down all that glory in the heavens to glean Our Saviour:*
  *And eyes, heart, what looks, what lips yet gave you a*
*Rapturous love's greeting of realer, of rounder replies?*

*And the azurous hung hills are his world-wielding shoulder*
  *Majestic—as a stallion stalwart, very-violet-sweet!—*
*These things, these things were here and but the beholder*
  *Wanting; which two when they once meet,*
*The heart rears wings bold and bolder*
  *And hurls for him, O half hurls earth for him off under his feet.*

Our eternal problem is how to make that bridge into the wonder of the living Oneness of God in nature. We are that part of nature which has achieved self-consciousness. We have gone through the experience of separation in order that, like the Prodigal Son, we can 'come to ourselves' and say "I will go back to my Father." Ultimately the human being is destined to become co-creator with God, having achieved freedom through separation. We approach the Aquarian age when human consciousness is able to take the step and know itself as one with the living wholeness. The great poets lead us into this knowledge.

Here is a remarkable illustration from the metaphysical poet Thomas Traherne. He possessed the faculty of remembering into the womb—and beyond, into pre-existence. His poems, written in the 17th century, were lost until they were rediscovered in an attic about 1900. How fittingly destiny works, for until that time nobody would have known what they were about! In this poem, *My Spirit*, he describes his experiences of being one with the realm of creative ideas. These verses are part of a longer poem:

*My essence was capacity*
*  That felt all things...*
*That made me present evermore*
*  With whatso'er I saw.*
*An object, if it were before*
*My eye, was by Dame Nature's law*
*  Within my soul.*
*O joy! O wonder and delight!*
*  O sacred mystery!*
*My soul a spirit infinite*
*An image of the Deity,*
*A pure substantial light,*
*  A strange mysterious sphere,*
*  A deep abyss*
*  That sees and is*
*The only proper place of Heavenly Bliss.*
*A strange extended orb of Joy*
*  Proceeding from within.*
*Which did on every side, convey*
*Itself, and being nigh of kin*
*  To God, did every way*
*Dilate itself even in an instant, and*

*Like an indivisible centre stand*
*At once surrounding all eternity.*

*O wondrous Self! O sphere of light,*
*    O sphere of joy most fair*
*O act, O power infinite;*
*    O subtile and unbounded air!*
*        O living orb of sight!*
*Thou which within me art, yet me! Thou eye,*
*And temple of His whole infinity!*
*    O what a world art Thou! A world within!*
*    All things appear, all objects are*
*Alive in Thee! Supersubstantial, rare,*
*    Above themselves, and nigh of kin*
*    To those pure things we find*
*        in His great mind*
*Who made the world! Tho' now eclipsed by sin,*
*    There they are useful and divine,*
*    Exalted there they ought to shine.*

These are the archetypal Ideas, which are strands of the Thought of God and are alive as the architects of every form. Traherne is talking about the inner centre we enter in meditation. Here is the pearl of great price, this secret chamber of the soul in which we can discover the radiant centre of light. This is a tremendous message. Realise that we are now concerned with the polar counterpart to space exploration. Everything works in polarity and today we are talking about inner space exploration, moving into what we must now call ethereal space. We discover within us an organ of inner sense and consciousness which moves faster than light, at the speed of thought, instantaneously. We are where we project our attention and therefore we can become an 'indivisible centre at once surrounding all eternity'. To quote William Blake, that great new age visionary:

*I rest not from my great task*
*To open the Eternal Worlds, to open the immortal Eyes*
*Of Man inwards into the Worlds of Thought, into Eternity,*
*Ever expanding in the Bosom of God, the Human Imagination.*

We understand in a new light the oriental doctrine 'That art Thou'.

We are all one, for the divinity in the tree is the same as the divinity in you and me. So Love floods us all. Rudolf Steiner, truly bridging scientific and spiritual knowledge, writes:

> *If we see in thinking the capacity to comprehend more than can be known to the senses, we are forced to recognise the existence of objects over and above those we experience in sense perception. Such objects are Ideas. In taking possession of the Idea, thinking merges itself into the World Mind. What was working without now works within. Man has become* one *with the World Being at its highest potency. Such a becoming-realised of the Idea is the true communion of man. Thinking has the same significance for Ideas as the eye for light and the ear for sound. It is an organ of perception.*

We have no time in this lecture to go into the doctrine of metamorphosis within plants and all nature, as presented by Goethe and developed by Steiner, which is vital for the imaginative understanding as to how living nature works. The artistry of nature is amazing, for she can allow forms to flow through metamorphosis and transform themselves, as seen in the transition from leaf into petal and stamen, and on into fruit and seed, that point of absolute formlessness into which the Idea can pour again. By observing this, Goethe arrived at the concept of the Archetypal Plant, the creative Being within all plant forms.

We learn to see that the Earth forces have the power to break down form so that it reverts to humus, the living soil. The forms of nature pour in from the realm of the creative Ideas, the ethereal world, to be broken down by dissolution into the matrix for the birth of new life. Thus we do well to meditate on those points where nature shows the grand and solemn music of dissolution and decay. I quote Wordsworth's fine sonnet *Mutability*:

> *From low to high doth dissolution climb,*
>    *And sink from high to low, along a scale*
>    *Of awful notes, whose concord shall not fail;*
> *A musical and melancholy chime,*
> *Which they can hear who meddle not with crime,*
>    *Nor avarice, nor over-anxious care.*
>    *Truth fails not; but her outward forms that bear*
> *The longest date do melt like frosty rime,*
> *That in the morning whitened hill and plain*

*And is no more; drop like the tower sublime*
  *Of yesterday, which royalty did wear*
*His crown of weeds, but could not even sustain*
  *Some casual shout that broke the silent air*
*Or the unimaginable touch of time.*

Now we begin to see what Wordsworth and Coleridge and the other poets of the Romantic movement were really saying. They faced the experience of modern consciousness losing touch with the oneness of life in nature. Here is the opening verse of Wordsworth's great *Ode on the Intimations of Immortality* in early childhood:

*There was a time when meadow, grove, and stream,*
  *The earth, and every common sight,*
    *To me did seem*
  *Apparelled in celestial light,*
*The glory and the freshness of a dream.*
*It is not now as it hath been of yore;—*
  *Turn whereso'er I may,*
    *By night or day,*
*The things which I have seen I now can see no more.*

  *The Rainbow comes and goes,*
  *And lovely is the Rose,*
  *The Moon doth with delight*
*Look round her when the heavens are bare,*
  *Waters on a starry night*
  *Are beautiful and fair;*
*The sunshine is a glorious birth*
*But yet I know, where'er I go*
*That there hath passed away*
  *A glory from the Earth.*
*Whither is fled the visionary gleam?*
*Where is it now, the glory and the dream?*

That glory, brought down by the child out of pre-existence, that infinity within the soul, is lost as we grow up and too often it is tacitly assumed that this dream is but the illusion of childhood. It is for us now to recover the 'vision splendid' and take the step in consciousness across the threshold of the spiritual world.

The great truth which the Romantic poets saw was that nature is not fulfilled until humankind takes this step in consciousness to unite with the being within form. We see why this planet is so infinitely important to the universe: the experiment of humanity awakening to a new birth is surely being watched from the angelic realms of higher intelligence. Coleridge expresses this thought in his *Dejection Ode*:

> *We receive but what we give,*
> *And in our life alone does Nature live:*
> *Ours is her wedding garment, ours her shroud!*
> *    And would we aught behold of higher worth,*
> *Than that inanimate cold world allowed*
> *To the poor loveless ever-anxious crowd,*
> *    Ah! from the soul itself must issue forth*
> *A light, a glory, a fair luminous cloud*
> *    Enveloping the Earth—*
> *And from the soul itself must there be sent*
> *    A sweet and potent voice, of its own birth,*
> *Of all sweet sounds the life and element.*

This is our task. I will draw to an end with an extraordinary little poem by Walt Whitman, from a group called *Whispers of Heavenly Death*. We know that all death is the passage through to renewal, to resurrection, to awakening. There can be no renewal without a dying process. In this poem 'heavenly death' is the opening into ethereal space, and the self talks to the soul:

> *Darest thou now O Soul*
> *Walk out with me towards the unknown region,*
> *Where neither ground is for the feet nor any path to follow?*
>
> *No map there, nor guide,*
> *Nor voice sounding, nor touch of human hand,*
> *Nor face with blooming flesh, nor lips, nor eyes are in that land.*
>
> *I know it not O Soul,*
> *Nor dost thou, all is blank before us,*
> *All waits undream'd of in that region, that inaccessible land.*
>
> *Till when the ties loosen*

*All but the ties eternal, Time and Space,*
*Nor darkness, gravitation, sense, nor any bounds bounding us.*

*Then we burst forth, we float,*
*In Time and Space, O Soul, prepared for them,*
*Equal, equipped at last (O Joy, O fruit of all)*
    *them to fulfil O Soul.*

Try to grasp that powerful thought: time and space itself is not fulfilled till human consciousness expands itself into it. We are the potential co-creator with God. We are the human archetype, the first in creation, and we are working up towards that archetype. This is not making extravagant claims for the significance of humankind, but it is recognising that the divine Idea which has developed upon planet Earth is of supreme importance to the whole of the universe. In this real sense nature, time and space are not fulfilled until we make that leap in consciousness into the poetical vision which marries science and mysticism. This is the step that will really bring us over the frontier into the Aquarian age. We are called upon to take it.